# HAVE YOURSELF A MOVIE LITTLE CHRISTMAS

ALSO BY ALONSO DURALDE

*101 Must-See Movies for Gay Men*

# Have Yourself a Movie Little Christmas

## ALONSO DURALDE

AN IMPRINT OF HAL LEONARD CORPORATION

NEW YORK

Published in 2010 by Limelight Editions
An Imprint of Hal Leonard Corporation
7777 West Bluemound Road
Milwaukee, WI 53213

Trade Book Division Editorial Offices
19 West 21st Street, New York, NY 10010

PHOTO CREDITS:
Front cover, clockwise from upper left: MGM/UA Entertainment/ Photofest, Twentieth Century-Fox Film Corporation/Photofest, Touchstone/Photofest, Photofest/Embassy Pictures Corporation, Warner Bros./Photofest; p. xiv: Paramount Pictures/Photofest; p. 2: NBC/Photofest; p. 18: Photofest; p. 52: Warner Bros./Photofest; p. 84: Odyssey Entertainment/Photofest; p. 102: Focus Features/Photofest; p. 124: Cinerama Releasing Corporation/Photofest; p. 142: NBC/Photofest; p. 174: Photofest/K. Gordon Murray Productions; p. 194: Photofest; p. 218: Dreamworks/Photofest; p. 232: MGM/Photofest

Printed in the United States of America
Book design by Mark Lerner

Library of Congress Cataloging-in-Publication Data

Duralde, Alonso.
Have yourself a movie little Christmas / by Alonso Duralde.
    p. cm.
Includes index.
ISBN 978-0-87910-376-7
1. Christmas films--Catalogs. I. Title.
PN1995.9.C5113D87 2010
016.79143'634--dc22
                          2010017998

ISBN 978-0-87910-376-7

www.limelighteditions.com

To Pilar Ampuero Duralde, for the ones I used to know

&

Dave White, for making life a perpetual spree

Kevin Spacey, Judy Davis, and Denis Leary in *The Ref* (1994).

# CONTENTS

**CHAPTER 2**

Nestled All Snug in Their Beds:

Christmas Movies for Grown Ups    19

**CHAPTER 3**

Like a Bowlful of Jelly: Christmas Comedies    53

**CHAPTER 8**

The Worst Christmas (Movies) Ever:
Lumps of Coal in Your Cinema Stocking

Bing Crosby, Rosemary Clooney, Danny Kaye, and Vera-Ellen in *White Christmas* (1954)

# Preface

When I was growing up, my family had a big Christmas dinner every year on the evening of December 24. My mother would always make her tasty marinated shrimp cocktail, and there would be a turkey and a ham and all sorts of delicious foods. And when you're a kid, you assume that your family does everything the correct and appropriate way.

As I got older, I realized that other families had traditions of their own. Most of them ate Christmas dinner on the 25th, whereas my parents, both born in Spain, were keeping the *Nochebuena* tradition from their own childhoods. Other families had prime rib or lamb or pork loin or—and I shudder to even type this—tofurkey.

But that's the great thing about Christmas; it's a time of year when we honor tradition, but everybody's traditions are different. Real tree or fake? Andy Williams or Elvis Presley? Eggnog or wassail? Snowflake sweater or antler hat? No two people celebrate the holiday in the same way, and it's that variety—and the possibility of adding a new tradition or two to your repertoire along the way—that makes Christmas a holiday that's both universal and very personal.

So it is with film: Say the phrase "Christmas movie" to someone, and he or she is likely to respond by citing *It's a Wonderful Life* or *A Christmas Story* or *Miracle on 34th Street*. But give that person an extra minute, and he or she will likely add, "You know, I've always thought of *Gremlins* as one of my favorite Christmas movies," or "Hey, have you ever seen *Lady in the Lake*?"

I love *White Christmas* as much as the next guy, but with this book I'm hoping to expand the definitions that people have for Christmas movies. When I enjoy the dark humor of *The Ref* or *La Bûche*, I get nostalgic for the very sarcastic (but way more functional) home in which I grew up. Even watching Bruce Willis as John McClane, putting everything on the line to rescue his estranged wife in *Die Hard*, gives me that glow that all great holiday-set redemption stories do. (And while I'm a total fraidy cat when it comes to horror movies, the original *Black Christmas* has somehow made its way onto my December screening list.)

It's never too late to discover a new Christmas favorite: My spouse showed me *Scrooge* (1970) for the first time when I was in my early 30s, and it instantly became my favorite screen adaptation of *A Christmas Carol*. More recently, Arnaud Desplechin's *A Christmas Tale* jumped on the list of movies I'm going to want to watch every December, so don't be surprised if some of the films contained herein shake up your traditional viewing habits.

Like all lists, this one is subjective and by no means complete, although I've tried to cover a broad range of films while also including the titles of plenty of other holiday movies in the appendix. Whether you're reading about films you already love or learning about new ones you might never have heard of, I hope this book entertains you and leads you toward movies that will bring you joy (in the form of laughs, tears, or screams) this Christmas.

Thanks for reading, and Happy Holidays!

# Acknowledgments

*It's a Wonderful Life* ends with George Bailey learning the measure of a man's wealth is in the friends that he makes, and the long and involved process of writing and publishing a book reminds me just how true that is.

For starters, this book would not be in your hands were it not for Eric Myers. I always wondered why people thanked their agents in awards-show acceptance speeches, but after working with Eric, I get it now. It was his unyielding belief in this project and his dogged efforts that took all of this from being a concept in the back of my mind to the published book it finally became.

Thanks also to everyone at Limelight Editions and Hal Leonard Publishing, particularly John Cerullo, Marybeth Keating, and Gary Morris, whose support and guidance has been invaluable throughout the process. A special shout-out as well to Ron Mandelbaum, Andrew McGovern, and Doug McKeown at Photofest—and photographer extraordinaire Gabriel Goldberg—for the photos that appear throughout.

Saving me from sounding like an idiot were my devoted crew of first-draft porer-overs, who brilliantly suggested improvements and corrections when all the sentences started blurring together for me: Robert Abele, Sean Abley, Charlotte Del Rose, Dennis Hensley, Jenni Olson, Mary Jo Pehl, Stephen Rebello, Margy Rochlin, and

Kim Usey were quick to pick up on any number of my factual and grammatical errors.

The staff at the Margaret Herrick Library of the Academy of Motion Picture Arts and Sciences and at the Paley Center for Media/ Los Angeles provided much-needed information and suggestions at every turn, as did the hard-working clerks at Rocket Video on La Brea Avenue in Hollywood. (Thanks for steering me to *The Silent Partner*, guys!) And I am forever indebted to Dave Kittredge and Rob McClary for putting together such extraordinary film-clip packages for both of my books.

Social networking has become vital to helping writers find a public, so I must thank all of my friends and readers at Facebook, Twitter, and Live Journal. And I'm eternally grateful to everyone whose kindness and friendship kept me sane through the process; I'm no doubt leaving some people out, but I must acknowledge the sheer awesomeness of Gariana Abeyta, Aaron Aldorisio, Ann Alexander, Kevin Bannerman, Hadrian Belove, Bret Berg, Phil Blankenship, Russell Boaz, John Cantwell, John Carroza, Danny Casillas, Mark Christopher, Dave Cobb (who came up with the title of this book), Tom Cohen, Ponny Joan Conomos, Gael Fashingbauer Cooper, Gary Cotti, Andrew Crane, Rafael Dalmau, Terry Danuser, Manohla Dargis, Grae Drake, Brett Erlich, Michele Fleury, Tom Ford, Ellen Fox, Bryan Fuller, Chris Gardner, Margot Gerber, Todd Gilchrist, Deven Green, Brad Griffith, Jason Havard, Marc Edward Heuck, Curt Holman, Stacie Hougland, Les Howell, Marcus Hu, Michael Jensen, Ari and Craig Karpel, Chuck Kim, Laura Kim, Paul Knepper, Bob Koenig, Chil Kong, Garrison Latimer (whose runner-up title for this book was too brilliant for words), Christy Lemire, Emanuel Levy, Steve Levy, Brian and Violet Lopes, Vinny Lopez, Leonard Maltin, Ben Mankiewicz, Lindsay Marsak, Amy Martin, Terence McFarland, Rosalinda Mendez, Matt Mishkoff, Jack Morrissey, "P. W." Mouradian, Bill Neil, Paige Newman, Shannon Leigh Olds, Jill Oliver, Jean Oppenheimer, Clark Parsons, Lisa Jane Persky, John

Polly, John Powers, Doug Prinzivalli, Kevin Quigley, Erin Quill, Loretta Ramos, Kurt B. Reighley, Scott Roberts, James Rocchi, Joal Ryan, Kirsten Schaffer, Jeffrey Schwarz, Brent Simon, Dennis Smeal, Ben Stein, Jeffrey Stewart, Sandi Tan, Tony Tripoli, Adam B. Vary, Louis Virtel, Judy Wieder, Michael Wilde, Jen Yamato, Kim Yutani, Andy Zax, and David Zeve.

I know that not everyone looks forward to the holiday season, and I want to express my gratitude to my family for making Christmas both a fond memory and a much-anticipated time of year. And since I have seven siblings, six terrific in-laws, and 15 nieces and nephews, I'm glad we've always been a draw-names-from-the-hat kind of clan.

My final can of Who Hash is for Dave White, who's my toughest critic and editor, the guy who keeps our household afloat when I'm having bad-movies-about-Santa-Claus marathons, and will always be the first face that I want to see on Christmas morning.

# HAVE YOURSELF A MOVIE LITTLE CHRISTMAS

# CHAPTER 1

Joan Cusack and her deeply felt co-stars in *It's a Very Merry Muppet Christmas Movie* (2002).

# With the Kids Jingle-Belling

## CHRISTMAS MOVIES FOR KIDS

There's never a bad time to expose kids to good movies. Showing them great films, whether it's the Marx Brothers or *The Wizard of Oz* (1939), is as important to their development as taking them to museums, and the holidays are ripe with great movie-watching opportunities. For one thing, there are lots of terrific holiday-themed films aimed at kids; for another, sitting them down in front of a good DVD for 90 minutes gives exhausted parents a rare bit of holiday respite. Take the opportunity to clean the kitchen, wrap some presents, or just sit down with a cup of Christmas-blend coffee or tea for some quiet time.

If you've got the time and the desire, of course, watching movies with kids can be entertaining and even educational. (Childhood viewings of *It's a Wonderful Life* [p. 202] provided me with an early lesson about banks, home loans, and the Great Depression.) This chapter features some entertaining movies for kids that won't drive their parents up the wall. And if you're a multitasking mom or dad, think of this as something the family can do together while you're updating the Christmas card list or knitting a scarf.

## *Ernest Saves Christmas* (1988)

PG; 95 min. Written by B. Kline and Ed Turner, based on a story by Ed Turner. Directed by John R. Cherry III. Starring Jim Varney, Douglas Seale, Oliver Clark, Noelle Parker. (Walt Disney Home Video)

Santa Claus (Seale) travels to Orlando to pass the reins—and his magic bag of toys—to his successor, nice-guy kiddie-show host Joe Curruthers (Clark). Joe, alas, thinks the old man claiming to be St. Nick is nuts; besides, he's considering other career options, namely a starring role in what turns out to be a cheesy and violent "family" film called *Christmas Slay*. Can rubber-faced cab driver Ernest P. Worrell (Varney) and teen runaway Harmony (Parker) help Santa convince his replacement to take over in time for Christmas? Or will Harmony's selfish exploration of the gift bag (to say nothing of Ernest's reckless driving of Santa's sleigh) keep the holiday from coming?

Varney created the character of Ernest P. Worrell in 1980 for a local TV commercial, and soon he was recording spots for clients all over the country. By the end of the decade, Ernest was starring in his own TV show (*Hey Vern, It's Ernest*) and in a series of popular films, including this one. Even if you have a limited tolerance for this hayseed goofball character, there are enough solidly funny bits in this film to make it terrific family viewing. (A solid supporting cast of comic second bananas, from Billie Bird to Gailard Sartain, helps matters along.) From Ernest and Harmony's destruction of the always-unseen Vern's home (in the process of hanging Christmas lights), to Ernest donning drag while pretending to be the cantankerous mother of Joe's obnoxious agent, *Ernest Saves Christmas* keeps the laughs coming while also supplying a warm fuzzy or two.

### FUN FACTS

- Varney's first big-screen appearance as Ernest was in the comedy *Dr. Otto and the Riddle of the Gloom Beam* (1986), but all subsequent films with the character had his name in the title: *Ernest Goes to Camp* (1987), *Ernest Scared Stupid* (1991), etc. The comedian also provided the voice of Slinky Dog in the first two *Toy Story* movies before his death in 2001 from lung cancer.

- *Ernest Saves Christmas* was the first feature film to be shot at what would later become the Disney-MGM Studios facility in Orlando. Ernest's house was a prominent feature on the studio tour until it was demolished in 2002.

## *Harry Potter and the Goblet of Fire* (2005)

PG-13 (for sequences of fantasy violence and frightening images); 157 min. Written by Steve Kloves, based on the novel by J. K. Rowling. Directed by Mike Newell. Starring Daniel Radcliffe, Emma Watson, Rupert Grint, Robert Pattinson. (Warner Home Video)

As though the return of the evil Lord Voldemort (Ralph Fiennes) wasn't already making his fourth year at Hogwarts School of Witchcraft and Wizardry difficult enough, young Harry Potter (Radcliffe) also finds himself forced to participate in the Triwizards Tournament, a demanding test of skill for magic students that attracts contenders from around the world. But perhaps the biggest challenge for Potter and his best friends Hermione (Watson) and Ron (Grint) is the prospect of finding dates for the school's annual Yule Ball. While *Goblet of Fire* goes to some dark places—the film features the first murder of a Hogwarts student at the hands of Voldemort—the Yule Ball sequence provides some much-needed light, as the school's Great Hall is transformed into a wintry paradise and the students get to ditch their wizarding robes for tuxedos and gowns. (Although poor Ron gets stuck with a hideous, ruffly hand-me-down.)

While there is a segment of the population that boycotts the *Harry Potter* novels and films because they supposedly promote the occult, this well-written series offers heroic young people taking up the cause of good and fighting off evil at all costs. And while *Goblet of Fire* might not seem like a holiday movie, the Yule Ball is one of the most—you'll pardon the expression—magical Christmas gatherings ever captured on film. If you live in a pro-Harry household, the holidays will be a perfect time to enjoy this fourth entry in the series, which is one of the most stirring and exciting chapters of the saga.

**FUN FACTS**

- Costume designer Jany Temime pulled out all the stops for the shooting of the Yule Ball, creating more than 300 new costumes for that sequence alone. A team of 100 dressmakers and wardrobe artists worked on gowns for the dance, with Hermione's dress alone requiring three months of work and a dozen yards of chiffon. "Hermione's dress had to be really special," said Temime. "I wanted it to be a fairy-tale dress, something that would make all the children gasp when she entered the room."

- Indie rock fans may recognize the members of the Weird Sisters, the band that plays the Yule Ball. They are Pulp's Jarvis Cocker and Steve Mackey, Johnny Greenwood and Phil Selway of Radiohead, Jason Buckle of All Seeing I, and Steve Claydon of Add N to (X). The band's name is a reference to the soothsaying witches who appear in Shakespeare's *Macbeth*.

## *Home Alone* (1990)

PG (cartoony violence); 103 min. Written by John Hughes. Directed by Chris Columbus. Starring Macaulay Culkin, Joe Pesci, Daniel Stern, Catherine O'Hara. (20th Century Fox Home Entertainment)

On the eve of his family's big Christmas trip to Paris, young Kevin (Culkin) gets on everyone's nerves, leading him to wish that he could be all alone, with no family to bother him. That desire comes true the next day when, through a series of mishaps, he gets left at home as everyone else takes off for Europe. While his frenzied mother (O'Hara) tries to hop a flight back to the States—because the phone lines at the house are knocked out, wouldn't ya know—two burglars (Pesci and Stern) try to take advantage of the holidays by robbing the neighborhood's vacated houses. The larcenous duo hasn't counted upon Kevin's ingeniousness in using household items (glass Christmas ornaments, paint cans, etc.) to booby-trap the place.

Released as just another family comedy at the end of 1990, *Home Alone* confounded even its own creators by becoming a smash hit, one that would outgross *Jaws* (1975) and *Return of the Jedi* (1983) to become, at that time, the third-highest-grossing movie ever released. It made a star of Macaulay Culkin (for a while, anyway) and led to a spate of films about clever suburban children inflicting grievous (but slapstick) bodily harm on adults. Decades later, however, the sequences showing the bad guys falling down and getting clonked on the head (and in various other anatomical locations) seem too realistic and sadistic to be funny, and Culkin's gleeful cries of "Yesssss!" every time he lays waste to one of his nemeses gets old fast. Still, while young audiences will love the physical humor, it's the movie's sentimentality that made it such a huge hit and a Christmas perennial. There's a lovely scene in which Kevin meets the neighborhood's scary old man (Roberts Blossom) in church during a choir rehearsal and discovers that the elderly gentleman isn't so creepy after all. *Home Alone* generally works more effectively at exploring the reality of the situation—a little kid's thrill in getting to eat junk food, ditching his crabby older siblings, and having full run of the house—than it does with the elaborate Rube Goldberg traps Kevin creates. Kevin's circumstances put him in league with the great Christmas heroes: His granted wish to be without a family gives Kevin a life lesson on par with George Bailey's and Ebenezer Scrooge's. All three get nightmarish glimpses at alternate lives, and when they return to their own existence, they appreciate what they already have and learn to value the people around them.

**FUN FACTS**

- That's actress Hope Davis—*American Splendor* (2003), *Synecdoche, New York* (2008)—making one of her first screen appearances as the not-very-helpful airline employee in the Paris airport.
- Several other holiday classics pop up in the film, including the TV special *How the Grinch Stole Christmas* and the films *It's a Wonderful Life* (p. 202; seen here dubbed into French) and *Miracle on 34th Street* (p. 207; Hughes would later write the 1996 remake).
- Warner Bros. passed on *Home Alone* when the budget climbed from $10 million to $17 million, thus depriving them of one of the all-time blockbusters. (That same year, Warner also passed on Tim Burton's *Edward Scissorhands* [p. 210], which wound up being another holiday hit for Fox.)
- Culkin was reportedly paid $110,000 for *Home Alone*, but his paycheck climbed to $4.5 million for the sequel, *Home Alone 2: Lost in New York* (1992).

## *It's a Very Merry Muppet Christmas Movie* (2002)

PG (for mild thematic elements; suitable for all ages); 100 minutes. Written by Tom Martin and Jim Lewis. Directed by Kirk R. Thatcher. Starring Kermit the Frog, Miss Piggy, Joan Cusack, David Arquette. (MGM Home Video)

It's Christmas Eve, and Kermit the Frog (voiced by Steve Whitmire) has lost all hope after the exceedingly cruel Rachel Bitterman (Cusack) of Bitterman Bank & Development—or BBAD—has taken away the lease to the Muppet Theater. Up in heaven, The Big Boss (Whoopi Goldberg) shows angel dispatcher Daniel (Arquette) how

Kermit arrived at this sorry state: Bitterman has used her wiles on Pepe the Prawn (Bill Barretta); Fozzie Bear (Eric Jacobson) faced a gauntlet of holiday hazards (he gets painted green in a tree-spraying machine, and then mistaken for the Grinch) while trying to deliver the deposit to BBAD on time; Miss Piggy (Jacobson) tackled a trapeze act while playing "Saltine" in an elaborate production number called *Moulin Scrooge!* When Daniel comes down to Earth to offer Kermit help, Kermit frets that he's made his friends waste their lives, and he wishes that he'd never been born. Armed with a copy of *Performing Miracles for Dummies*, Daniel grants Kermit's wish, showing him a world where Gonzo (Dave Goelz) is a street performer, Dr. Teeth and the Electric Mayhem perform Celtic dance, Fozzie is a pickpocket, and crazy cat lady Miss Piggy runs a phony psychic hotline. When Gonzo sings a depressing Christmas song—one that actually makes fun of how depressing it is—Kermit sees the light and returns to his life, ready to fight for everything he's built.

Any similarities to *It's a Wonderful Life* (p. 202) are, of course, completely intentional, but this riotously funny Muppet movie is more than just a spoof of that particular Christmas classic. While the film takes aim at any number of other holiday stories (see below), *Very Merry* reminds us that families aren't always just the people to whom we're biologically related. Fans of the Muppets have seen this frog, this pig, this bear, this . . . whatever Gonzo is, and all of their friends form their own unique family. And we honor that family of choice at the holidays as much as we do our own relatives. As one character so pointedly notes, "If you can help friends—and get revenge on your enemies—isn't that what Christmas is all about?"

**FUN FACTS**

- Among the Christmas perennials that get mocked here are the *Rudolph the Red-Nosed Reindeer* TV special (a snowman and would-be narrator gets knocked out with a tranquilizer dart), O. Henry's "Gift of the Magi," and *A Christmas Story* (p. 199), among others. The film also skewers Hong Kong martial-arts movies (Cusack and Miss Piggy face off for battle, and their badly dubbed dialogue doesn't match the movement of their lips).

- In the "world without Kermit" sequence, there's a Doc Hopper's French-Fried Frog Legs stand, a reference to the sinister restaurant chain owned by the villain of the original *The Muppet Movie* (1979).

## *Little Women* (1994)

**PG (suitable for all ages); 115 min. Written by Robin Swicord, based on the novel by Louisa May Alcott. Directed by Gillian Armstrong. Starring Winona Ryder, Susan Sarandon, Trini Alvarado, Christian Bale. (Sony Pictures Home Entertainment)**

The March family weathers trying times while Father is off fighting the Civil War. Marmee (Sarandon) rules the house with a firm but loving hand, raising four bright daughters—practical Meg (Alvarado), imaginative Jo (Ryder), compassionate Beth (Claire Danes), and flighty Amy (Kirsten Dunst, then later Samantha Mathis). Jo writes swashbuckling melodramas that she and her sisters act out with the help of neighbor boy Laurie (Bale), and she eventually becomes a writer. Beth's care for a local immigrant family leads to her lifelong battles with poor health, while Amy pursues her dreams of being an artist. Throughout everything, it is their family bond that keeps them together.

It's so very rare to get a big-budget Hollywood movie that highlights strong, independent women whose love and care nurture each other and, eventually, the men in their lives, but that's just one reason why this adaptation of the Alcott novel deserves to be cherished. While it's a movie that can be watched at any time of year, this version of *Little Women* offers two unforgettable Christmas scenes—one where the March girls sacrifice their cherished Christmas breakfast of sausage, oranges, bread, and butter for a starving family, and a later episode where Laurie's crusty grandfather (John Neville) gives Beth his beautiful piano. (Young Danes, fresh off her breakthrough role in TV's *My So-Called Life*, gives an unabashedly poignant performance as brave, doomed Beth.)

**FUN FACTS**

- Screenwriter Swicord used elements of Alcott's real life—including her interest in Transcendentalism and racial equality—in adapting the classic novel.
- Australian director Armstrong at first turned down *Little Women*, fearing that part of the story—Jo turning down Laurie's marriage proposal so that she may pursue her writing—was too similar to the plot of her acclaimed directorial debut *My Brilliant Career* (1979). Once she accepted the job, Armstrong immediately began reading up on the American Civil War, about which she knew very little.
- Mary Wickes, as the formidable Aunt March, made her final film appearance here after nearly 60 years on the big screen. The veteran character actress is recognizable from her work in *White Christmas* (p. 214), *Sister Act* (1992), *The Trouble With Angels* (1966), and *Now, Voyager* (1942), among countless other films and TV shows.

## *Millions* (2004)

PG (for thematic elements, language, some peril, and mild sensuality; suitable for kids 6 and up); 98 minutes. Written by Frank Cottrell Boyce. Directed by Danny Boyle. Starring Alex Etel, Lewis McGibbon, James Nesbitt. (20th Century Fox Home Entertainment)

For young Damian (Etel) and his brother Anthony (McGibbon), it's their first Christmas in their new house and also their first without their recently departed mum. But things are about to get a whole lot more complicated. While playing in his cardboard-box fort by the railroad tracks and having a conversation with St. Clare of Assisi, the patron saint of television, Damian—whose obsession with the Catholic saints, particularly since his mother's passing, makes him see them all the time—finds a bag full of money that's been chucked out of a passing train. Damian wants to give the cash to the poor, while Anthony's head swims with the financial possibilities. Whatever the two decide to do with the money, however, they're going to have to do it quickly, since they're just days away from the New Year, when Britain converts to the Euro and all pound notes will become worthless. And if all that weren't difficult enough, the criminal who tossed the bag from the train starts sniffing around looking for it.

A huge change of pace for director Boyle—the man behind *Slumdog Millionaire* (2008) had, to that point, been best known for gritty films like *Trainspotting* (1996) and *28 Days Later* (2002)— and screenwriter Boyce—*24 Hour Party People* (2002), *Welcome to Sarajevo* (1997)—*Millions* is a charming and eccentric tale of youngsters getting through their grief while facing a decidedly hairy situation. It's the kind of movie that understands the unease of the first day of school, the infinite pleasures of a large cardboard box, and even the capacity of kids to use "Our mum's dead" as a get-out-of-jail-free card. Damian is a rare creation—saintly (literally) but never sanctimonious, he communes with the Catholic martyrs mainly so he can ask them if they've run into his mother in Heaven. Anthony's larceny ("It isn't the money's fault if it's stolen") plays realistically and not as an exaggerated plot twist, while even the local Mormon missionaries have a hard time embracing asceticism in the face of consumer electronics anonymously donated by Damian. *Millions* tells you everything you want to hear about love, family, and generosity at Christmastime without ever beating you over the head with it.

**FUN FACTS**

- The original screenplay was set in 1976, but the story was moved to the modern day to give the plot a "ticking clock" element with the Euro changeover (which has yet to actually take place in the United Kingdom).
- How did Boyce come by his keen ear for the language of children? Maybe being the father of seven helped.

## *Prancer* (1989)

**G; 103 minutes. Written by Greg Taylor. Directed by John Hancock. Starring Rebecca Harrell, Sam Elliott, Cloris Leachman. (MGM Home Entertainment)**

Like the hero of *Millions*, young Jessica Riggs (Harrell) is coping with her family's first Christmas after her mother's death; her afterlife obsessions are centered on just one saint in particular, however—Santa Claus. (By Jessica's figuring, if there's no Santa, then what if there's no God? And if there's no God, that means there's no heaven, and then where did her mother go after she died?) While her father (Elliott) is doing his best to keep the family together and to save his apple orchard from foreclosure, Jessica discovers an injured reindeer, and she's just positive that it's Prancer, one of Santa's team of sleigh pullers. While her father wants to shoot the animal, and the local vet (Abe Vigoda) thinks she's crazy to try to save the reindeer, Jessica forges on determinedly. (She's the kind of girl who, her father notes, "plays Christmas records all year.") Even if she has to do chores for the town's mean old rich lady (Leachman) to afford food for her new friend, Jessica will face any obstacles necessary to reunite Prancer with Santa Claus.

Some holiday movies—the wretched *One Magic Christmas* (1985) and the overbearing *The Polar Express* (2004) to name just two— get so strident about the idea of believing in Santa Claus, lest you become a black-hearted curmudgeon, that they turn off audiences and paint themselves into philosophical corners. But Jessica's *need* to believe in Santa and everything he represents makes her a fascinating character, particularly since Harrell is such a natural and appealing screen presence. *Prancer's* plot takes lots of interesting turns, but it never strains the plausibility of what might happen in a small town if one of Santa's reindeer showed up one Christmas. (It gets details like sledding hills—and a holiday pageant whose nativity scene somehow includes snow, leopards, and chickens—just right.) A *Field of Dreams* (1989) with antlers, *Prancer* avoids being treacly, although you should get your eyes checked if they don't mist up at least a little bit when Elliott reads "Yes, Virginia, There is a Santa Claus" to his screen daughter.

**FUN FACTS**
- Director John Hancock shot the film in LaPorte, Ind., his hometown. Temperatures dropped as low as 42 below zero during shooting.
- Boo, the reindeer who plays Prancer, was pregnant for most of the production. When she gave birth, the baby was named Raffaella in honor of *Prancer* producer Raffaella de Laurentiis.

## *The Santa Clause* (1994)

PG (a few crude moments; 6 and up); 97 min. Written by Leo Benvenuti and Steve Rudnick. Directed by John Pasquin. Starring Tim Allen, Wendy Crewson, Judge Reinhold, Eric Lloyd. (Walt Disney Home Video)

Toy company executive and divorced dad Scott Calvin (Allen) can't get his holiday act together, injuring himself in the attempt to make Christmas dinner for his recalcitrant son Charlie (Lloyd). (They wind up at Denny's with all the other single dads, sporting bandages from their culinary efforts.) That night, Scott hears someone on his roof and assumes it's a burglar, but it's Santa Claus. Startled by Scott,

Santa falls off and hits the ground. Scott puts on the suit, and he and Charlie wind up making Santa's deliveries for him. When they arrive at the North Pole, Scott is informed that by putting on the red suit he has activated "the Santa Clause," a contract which states that he has one year to prepare for becoming the new St. Nicholas. While Scott tries to fight off the belly and snow-white beard that suddenly appear, Charlie worries his mother Laura (Crewson) and her psychiatrist husband Neil (Reinhold) with all his talk about flying reindeer and toy-making elves. Will Scott be ready to become Santa in time for December 24? And can Charlie ever make Laura and Neil believe that his dad is Father Christmas?

Lots of movies have gotten Santa wrong—tales of the Man in Red dominate this book's chapter about the best worst Christmas movies (p. 175)—but *The Santa Clause* deftly balances childlike faith and wonder with a gently snarky modern sensibility. (David Krumholtz's deadpan elf bridges this gap perfectly.) It's a movie that's not afraid to linger over the day-to-day details of what would happen to a man who finds out he's about to inherit the mantle of one of the world's most beloved figures—interesting explanations are provided as to how Santa can cover the world in one night and squeeze into houses that don't even have chimneys—and Allen gives one of his finest performances as a holiday cynic who suddenly finds kids lining up to sit on his lap to ask for presents. (And if you love puns, there's no resisting a movie with the line, "Out on the lawn, there's a Rose Suchak Ladder.") *The Santa Clause* was followed by two sequels: *The Santa Clause 2* (2002) is more fun than *The Santa Clause 3: The Escape Clause* (2006), but you'll be just fine sticking with the original.

**FUN FACTS**

- If you play close attention, you'll spot many elves throughout the film in the non–North Pole sequences of Scott and Charlie's day-to-day life. These stealth elves all gather at a significant moment late in the film.

- Director Pasquin had previously worked with Allen on the hit sit-com *Home Improvement*; they would reunite less successfully for the critically drubbed *Jungle 2 Jungle* (1997).

## *Unaccompanied Minors* (2006)

PG (for mild rude humor and language); 90 minutes. Written by Jacob Meszaros and Mya Stark. Directed by Paul Feig. Starring Dyllan Christopher, Gia Mantegna, Tyler James Williams, Lewis Black. (Warner Home Video)

Winter storms trap a whole bunch of children traveling alone—"unaccompanied minors," in airline-speak—on Christmas Eve at Hoover International Airport. Spencer (Christopher) leads a group of kids who escape the bunker-like "U.M. Room" and explore the airport—Grace (Mantegna) enjoys a spa treatment, Charlie (Williams, at that time the star of TV's *Everybody Hates Chris*) takes a spin on the Sharper Image karaoke machine, Donna (Quinn Shephard) hijacks a people-mover, and Beef (Brett Kelly from *Bad Santa*, p. 22) inflates some emergency landing gear, while Spencer has a junk food extravaganza in the airport restaurant. When Oliver Porter (Lewis Black), the airport's crabby "passenger relations manager who doesn't like passengers," forcibly takes them back to the room, they discover that all of the other kids have been sent to a nearby hotel for the night. Spencer must devise a way for them to bring his younger sister Katie (Dominique Saldaña) a doll, lest she think that Santa has forgotten her. But will Katie survive her night with a bratty, makeover-obsessed pre-teen? Will Spencer and Katie's dad (Rob Corddry) make it to the airport in his eco-friendly, vegetable-oil–fueled car? And can the kids outsmart Mr. Porter and help him learn to love Christmas again?

While *Unaccompanied Minors* reads very much as a post–*Home Alone* (p. 6) movie, it has its own appeal independent of that prior megahit. Director Feig created *Freaks and Geeks*, one of TV's greatest comedy-dramas, and his gift for casting new faces and eliciting strong performances from young actors is very much in evidence here. While there's a poignant undercurrent to the film—all of the main characters are children of divorce, which makes them slightly ambivalent about the holidays and also, as Spencer notes, "more resourceful"—the laughs keep coming. Teri Garr has a great bit as a Christmas-obsessed woman with lawn decorations so aggressive they actually frighten passersby, while a parade of great contemporary comedians (see below) keep popping up in various roles, both large and small. *Unaccompanied Minors* fell between the cracks during its all-too-brief theatrical release, but here's hoping that it finds its audience on DVD.

## FUN FACTS

- *Unaccompanied Minors* began life as a story by Susan Burton on the public radio show *This American Life*, about having to spend a night in a hotel with strangers when she and her younger sister were snowed in during air travel. Burton later noted, "When I imagined the movie of my life, I never thought I would be portrayed by a teenage boy."
- Feig rounded up an amazing array of comic talent for the film's supporting characters, including three of the Kids in the Hall (playing airport security guards in, of course, a hall), various cast members from *The Daily Show* (Black, Corddry, Rob Riggle, David Koechner), author and NPR commentator Sandra Tsing Loh, *The Office*'s Mindy Kaling and B. J. Novak, *Arrested Development*'s Jessica Walter and Tony Hale, *Saturday Night Live*'s Kristen Wiig, *Reno 911!*'s Cedric Yarbrough, and *Freaks and Geeks*' Dave "Gruber" Allen.

# CHAPTER 2

Jean-Louis Trintignant and Françoise Fabian in *My Night at Maud's* (*Ma nuit chez Maud*) (1969).

# Nestled All Snug in Their Beds

## MOVIES FOR GROWN-UPS

People often think of Christmas as a holiday that's just for kids, but the joys of the season continue to resonate throughout our lives. I've had a blast waking up early on December 25th and watching my nieces and nephews tear into their gifts, but even if I'm at home with my own family, we put up a tree and decorate the house and drink eggnog and observe all the holiday traditions even though there are no little ones to be found.

And so, lest you think that all Christmas movies are aimed at the young'uns, here are some great ones meant for mature audiences. From dark comedies about families whose dysfunctions bubble up to the surface during the holidays to intense dramas that use the bright and shining season as a counterpoint to serious matters, there's no shortage of compelling films you'll want to catch after the children have gone to sleep or are otherwise occupied. I've even thrown in a documentary that's probably too slowly paced for young viewers but that provides a fascinating glimpse at that most universal of Christmastime activities: shopping.

## *The Apartment* (1960)

Unrated; 125 min. Written by Billy Wilder and I. A. L. Diamond. Directed by Billy Wilder. Starring Jack Lemmon, Shirley MacLaine, Fred MacMurray, Ray Walston. (MGM Home Video)

C. C. Baxter (Lemmon) is a corporate drone looking to get ahead at the Consolidated Life of New York insurance company, so he loans the key to his apartment to various executives who use the place to entertain young ladies to whom they are not married. Baxter maintains a polite flirtation with elevator operator Fran Kubelik (MacLaine), not knowing that she's the girl that powerful head of personnel Jeff Sheldrake (MacMurray) is taking to the apartment. When Baxter learns the truth, he's devastated, but he's barely got time to deal with his feelings before coming home to find that Fran has swallowed a bottle of pills after realizing that Sheldrake is never going to leave his wife for her. Over the Christmas holiday, Baxter nurses Fran back to health, while an embittered ex-girlfriend of Sheldrake's tells his wife everything: Now that he's available again, will Sheldrake win Fran back, or will she realize that Baxter's the man for her?

Billy Wilder is one of our greatest cinematic wits, but there's an undercurrent of melancholy and loneliness that suffuses even the lightest moments of this multiple Oscar-winner. Fran Kubelik ranks among the saddest and most damaged characters that the ebullient MacLaine ever played—when Baxter notices the mirror in her compact is cracked, she replies, "I like it that way. Makes me look the way I feel."—and she gets it just right, revealing the fire that makes her attractive to men and the deep sorrow that lurks just under it. Like *Desk Set* (p. 60), the film provides a glimpse into the long-gone white-collar world of bacchanalian Christmas parties, where male executives were given free range to fanny-pinch their female underlings. Baxter's sad little Christmas tree provides ironic counterpoint to Fran's attempted suicide, but it also provides a glimmer of hope for two people who desperately need it.

## FUN FACTS

- Wilder filmed the Christmas party sequence on December 23, 1959, in the hopes of taking advantage of the cast's holiday spirits. The result is one of the most raucous holiday parties ever captured on film—and Wilder got most of it on the first take.
- Much of the film's dialogue, including its famous last line, was actually improvised on set. Wilder gave MacLaine a forty-page screenplay because he didn't want her to know what happened to her character until they were actually filming.
- There are several self-referential moments in the film, from Mr. Kirkeby (David Lewis) describing Bud and Fran having "a lost weekend"—Wilder's film adaptation of *The Lost Weekend* (1945), like *The Apartment*, won a Best Picture Oscar—to Mr. Dobisch (Walston) picking up a girl who "looks just like Marilyn Monroe"—Monroe had starred in Wilder's *The Seven Year Itch* (1955) and *Some Like It Hot* (1959). Wilder also featured characters named Sheldrake in *Sunset Blvd.* (1950) and *Kiss Me, Stupid* (1964).
- *The Apartment* was the last black and white movie to win a Best Picture Oscar until *Schindler's List* (1993).
- This film was later turned into the 1969 Burt Bacharach-Hal David Broadway musical *Promises, Promises* (revived in 2010), which featured choreography by Michael Bennett and a book by Neil Simon.
- Set designer Alexandre Trauner used false perspective to make the vast insurance office look bigger—in reality, the desks get smaller and smaller as they get further from the camera, and little people played office workers in the back of the shot.

## *Bad Santa* (2003)

**R; 88/91/98 min. Written by John Ficarra and Glenn Requa. Directed by Terry Zwigoff. Starring Billy Bob Thornton, Tony Cox, Brett Kelly, Lauren Graham. (Miramax Home Entertainment)**

Every Christmas, Willie (Thornton) and Marcus (Cox) work the same scam—they get jobs as Santa and elf in a department store, and then on Christmas Eve, they rob the place. But Willie is a self-destructive alcoholic, and it's affecting his safecracking skills. In Phoenix, they work their setup again, but things go awry. For one thing, goofy kid Thurman Merman (Kelly) becomes obsessed with Santa/Willie, and Willie finds himself trying to teach the boy how to make his way in the world without suffering daily wedgies. To make matters worse, mall security chief Gin (Bernie Mac) figures out their scam and demands half of the take. Can Willie stay sober enough to do the job? Will his propensity for loud sex with women in the big-and-tall changing rooms get him fired by nebbishy mall manager Bob (John Ritter)? And why does Thurman's dotty grand-mother (an uncredited Cloris Leachman) keep making sandwiches for everyone?

Conceived (and executive-produced) by Joel and Ethan Coen, *Bad Santa* holds nothing sacred; Thornton's Willy isn't a funny, charming tippler—he's a barely functioning drunk. He swears in front of children, wets himself, has loud sex with Santa-obsessed bar-tender Sue (Graham)—who yells hilarious profanities throughout their encounters—and plans to rob his place of employment. This, in other words, is not the Santa of *Miracle on 34th Street* (p. 207); the film does everything it can to subvert the idea of Christmas movies as being sentimental and life-affirming. (Subsequently, *Bad Santa* has both fervent fans and ardent detractors. I'm admittedly on the fence, but I admire the film's commitment to what it wants to do.) If you're in the right mindset for the naughty and scabrous humor on display here, though, *Bad Santa* will become your annual antidote to seasonal sweetness and light.

**FUN FACTS**

- There are three versions of *Bad Santa* floating around: The original theatrical cut runs 91 minutes, the "Badder Santa" DVD (prepared without input from director Terry Zwigoff) includes extra scenes for a total of 98 minutes, and Zwigoff's director's-cut version is a stripped-down 88 minutes. Why is the director's cut shortest? It takes out almost every moment where Willie shows any measure of affection for Thurman; it's the darkest version, but apparently the one truest to the filmmaker's original vision.
- *Bad Santa* featured John Ritter's final performance in a live-action film; he and Thornton had previously worked together on the TV series *Hearts Afire* and in Thornton's feature directorial debut, *Sling Blade* (1996).
- The final safe that Willis cracks is a Kitnerboy Redoubt; there's no such safe, but it's assumed that the name is a reference to "that little Kintner boy," one of the victims in *Jaws* (1975).

# *The Box* (2009)

**R; 113 min. Written by Richard Kelly, based on the story "Button, Button" by Richard Matheson. Directed by Richard Kelly. Starring Cameron Diaz, James Marsden, Frank Langella. (Warner Home Video)**

The week before Christmas 1976, as NASA's Viking mission is landing on Mars, married couple Norma (Diaz) and Arthur Lewis (Marsden) have just been dealt financial setbacks at their respective jobs as schoolteacher and NASA researcher, making them all too vulnerable for an experiment being conducted by the mysterious Arlington Steward (Langella). He delivers a box with a big red button to their house early one morning, and he returns later to explain to them how it works: If they press the button, the Lewises will receive one million dollars. However, someone, somewhere, whom they don't know, will die. They have 24 hours to decide. The arrival of the mysterious box is just the beginning of the Lewises' terrifying journey into paranoia, extraterrestrial activity, and the most difficult decisions they will ever face as parents.

Richard Kelly made a big splash with his directorial debut, *Donnie Darko* (2001), but his legions of fans were genuinely baffled by his dreamlike and impenetrable follow-up, *Southland Tales* (2006). *The Box*, based on a Richard Matheson story that had previously been the basis of a *Twilight Zone* episode, was meant to reestablish Kelly as a commercial filmmaker, but most audiences and critics found themselves equally perplexed. Having not been a fan of *Southland Tales*, I was surprised to find myself riveted by *The Box*: Unlike 99% of most movies released by major studios, the film is completely unpredictable and fascinatingly enigmatic—several viewings later, you'll probably still be trying to put all of its pieces together. (And if you think you know what's going to happen because you saw the *Twilight Zone* version, that part of the story occupies only about the first third of the movie.) Diaz gives a captivating and mature performance, and Langella's cold creepiness steals every scene he's in; his unsettling screen presence is made all the more so thanks to a combination of makeup and special effects that make it look like half his face is missing. It's haunting and perplexing, but once you open *The Box*, you'll find it's an experience that's hard to shake.

**FUN FACTS**

- The composers of the film's haunting score are best known for their work in indie bands: Win Butler and Régine Chassagne are the founders of the Arcade Fire, and Owen Pallett is the principal member of Final Fantasy.

- Kelly's father was a NASA engineer on the Viking mission. While Kelly's childhood memories of his father's job certainly color the film, it also led to a more tangible benefit—the director was given permission to shoot at Langley Air Force Base and NASA Langley Research Center in Hampton, Va., two locations that had never before permitted a film production.
- Early in the development process, Eli Roth (*Hostel*) collaborated with Kelly on the screenplay; he is not credited on the final script.
- Attentive Kelly fans will note actress Lisa K. Wyatt, who plays a reporter in *The Box*; she first worked with the director on his thesis film and subsequently appeared in all of his features.

## *Brazil* (1985)

R; 142 min. (director's cut). Written by Terry Gilliam, Tom Stoppard, and Charles McKeown. Directed by Terry Gilliam. Starring Jonathan Pryce, Katherine Helmond, Kim Greist, Robert De Niro. (Universal Home Video/The Criterion Collection)

Sam Lowry (Pryce) is a bureaucrat in an Orwellian police state, but in his dreams, he's a winged warrior in love with a beautiful blonde woman. The appearance of Jill (Greist), a dead ringer for his dream girl, inspires Sam to get promoted so he can have access to information about where to find her, but the higher he goes in the government, the more horrible truths he uncovers about how his world really works. Meanwhile, he's got to cope with his mother (Helmond) and her unending desire for extensive plastic surgery, the mountains of paperwork involved in getting his air conditioning fixed, and the appearance of notorious plumber-terrorist Harry Tuttle (De Niro), who's fighting the system.

Gilliam's greatest work post–Monty Python is this dark and visually extravagant satire set in a world that seems simultaneously retro and futuristic. He threads bizarre Christmas imagery throughout, from Sam's bathroom encounter with his Santa-clad boss to the partially unwrapped gifts he's constantly being given. Once you've seen the film, take the time to dig through the Criterion DVD's many extras, including the absurdly optimistic version of Gilliam's bleak tale that Universal Pictures wanted to release—it's a fascinating lesson in art vs. commerce.

See also: Two earlier films co-directed by Gilliam also contain hilariously askew visions of Christmas: *Monty Python's Life of Brian* (1979) opens with its hero being born in the stable next door to the one where Jesus lies in a manger, and *Monty Python's Meaning of Life* (1983) closes with an extravagant "Christmas in Heaven" number, which suggests the afterlife will be chock-full of consumer goodies and popular franchise films.

**FUN FACTS**

- Sheila Reid, who plays Mrs. Buttle, later turned up as Scrooge's housekeeper in the TV movie *A Christmas Carol: The Musical* (p. 154).

- The password "Ere I am, JH" is an anagram of "Jeremiah," Sam's father's name.

- Gilliam's battles with Universal Studios exec Sid Sheinberg over which version of the film to release were legendary: Gilliam appeared on *Good Morning America* and flashed a photo of Sheinberg while complaining about how the film was being treated; later, Gilliam took out a full-page ad in *Variety* asking when Sheinberg would release his film. It wasn't until the Los Angeles Film Critics Association voted the Gilliam cut as Best Picture of the Year—before either version of *Brazil* had actually played in theaters—that Universal finally capitulated. (Jack Mathews' riveting book *The Battle of Brazil* thoroughly details Gilliam's travails with Universal over the film.)

# La Bûche (1999)

**Unrated; 106 min. Written by Danièle Thompson and Christopher Thompson. Directed by Danièle Thompson. Starring Emmanuelle Béart, Charlotte Gainsbourg, Sabine Azéma, Claude Rich. (Fox Lorber Home Video)**

Christmas is coming, but for one French family with three adult daughters, there's nothing to get excited about. Sonia (Béart) is busting her hump to put on the perfect Christmas dinner, but no one particularly appreciates her efforts, least of all her philandering husband. (Sonia has her own thing going on the side with a sexy grocer.) Singer Louba (Azéma) can't get her married lover to leave his wife, and the surly Milla (Gainsbourg) has always despised Christmas. (The *bûche* Christmas cake of the title, she says, "makes me want to throw up.") Over the course of getting ready for 25 Decembre, however, all their lives will change—at least partially due to the sudden appearance of a handsome stranger (Christopher Thompson)—and even the sisters' long-battling parents Stanislas (Rich) and Yvette (Françoise Fabian) may figure out how to be civil to one another.

*La Bûche* immediately tips its hand as a Christmas movie for people who hate Christmas; the credits roll over shots of garishly decorated Paris streets, with a chorus of French singers shrieking "Jingle Bells" in English on the soundtrack. In the very first scene, Yvette buries her second husband, only to have the funeral interrupted by the ringing of a cell phone, which is, as it turns out, inside the casket—the man's mistress is calling, because Yvette didn't bother to tell her of his passing. And so it goes. But while there's plenty of hilarious tartness to the film, it also reveals a hidden sweet center, particularly when the characters reminisce about Christmases past (ranging from Stanislas' moving childhood memory of being a Jewish refugee to Milla's revelation of why the holiday bothers her so).

**FUN FACTS**

- This was the directorial debut of French screenwriter Danièle Thompson, best known in the U.S. for the provocative romantic comedy *Cousin, Cousine* (1975). She co-wrote the screenplay for *La Bûche* with her son Christopher, who plays mysterious boarder Joseph. The director said of the film, "Those who like it would like me, too. The others wouldn't like me. The movie is too much like me."

- Fabian's previous stint in a Christmas-themed comedy was in Eric Rohmer's *My Night at Maud's* (p. 44).

## *Christmas Holiday* (1944)

Unrated; 93 min. Written by Herman J. Mankiewicz, based on the novel by W. Somerset Maugham. Directed by Robert Siodmak. Starring Deanna Durbin, Gene Kelly, Dean Harens, Richard Whorf. (Not available on DVD in the United States)

Newly minted officer Lt. Charles Mason (Harens) gets dumped by his fiancée via a "Dear John" letter but decides to travel to San Francisco to confront her. Rain forces his plane down in New Orleans; at the hotel, he meets shady journalist Simon Fenimore (Whorf), who takes him to the Maison Lafitte, a local nightclub. (The club is clearly meant to be a bordello; the production code allowed filmmakers to suggest this but not to come out and say so.) There, Charles hears Jackie (Durbin) sing a torch song; the two dance, and she asks him to take her to midnight mass. Toward the end of the service, when everyone sings "Adeste Fideles," Jackie bursts into tears. Charlie takes her out to a diner, and she pours out her life story—she loved Robert (Kelly), a mother-obsessed gambler who went to jail for killing a bookie. While Jackie tells Charles about her past, Robert has broken out of prison. And he's looking for her.

Deanna Durbin and Gene Kelly are two of the last people you would imagine starring in a twisty 1940s film noir thriller—in 1944, Kelly was in the process of becoming one of MGM's most legendary song-and-dance men, while Durbin was taking on her first adult film role after nearly a decade of successfully playing juvenile leads in light comedies like *Three Smart Girls* (1936). (Durbin's reign as a child star is often credited with keeping Universal out of bankruptcy in the 1930s.) Even though they're cast very much against type, both stars are just as comfortable in the nihilistic world of noir as they were singing with Judy Garland. After the shock of seeing these performers out of their usual context recedes, you'll be gripped by this brooding and haunting tragedy. Part psychological drama and part bleak holiday tale, *Christmas Holiday* merits a U.S. DVD release so that more viewers can experience this little-remembered but vividly unusual film.

## FUN FACTS

- In the original Maugham story, the lead character is a Russian prostitute in Paris whose husband has been sent to Devil's Island; she tells her story to an upper-class Brit.
- Screenwriter Mankiewicz co-wrote Orson Welles' *Citizen Kane* (1941), another film told almost entirely in flashbacks.
- Durbin later called *Christmas Holiday* her favorite of her films; she didn't want to sing in it, but the studio insisted. Her big number, "Spring Will Be a Little Late This Year," was written by Frank Loesser; she and Kelly also sing Irving Berlin's "Always." The film won an Oscar for Hans J. Salter's score.

# A Christmas Tale (Un Conte de Noël) (2008)

Unrated; 150 min. Written by Arnaud Desplechin and Emmanuel Bourdieu. Directed by Arnaud Desplechin. Starring Catherine De-

**neuve, Mathieu Amalric, Melvil Poupaud, Chiara Mastroianni. (The Criterion Collection)**

The Vuillard family is once again gathering for Christmas in the dingy industrial town of Roubaix, but this reunion is anything but business as usual. For one thing, Junon (Deneuve) is dying of a bone marrow disease that is untreatable unless one of her family members is enough of a genetic match for transplant. (With this disease, it's customary for parents to be donors to their sick children, but Junon figures that she gave her kids life, so they can at least return the favor.) This Christmas also marks the return of Henri (Amalric) to the family fold, after he had been banished by his sister Elisabeth (Anne Consigny) after a crooked business deal that went wrong. Amidst the festivities, some members of the Vuillard clan revive old grudges while others find love, learn surprising truths, and attempt to understand the baffling and gratifying bonds of family.

It's nearly impossible to do justice to this funny, heartbreaking, and provocative film with a simple plot synopsis; Desplechin loads in so many conflicted characters, familial relationships (that run the gamut from loving to prickly to combinations thereof), literary and cinematic references (encompassing everything from Nietzsche to Cecil B. DeMille's *The Ten Commandments*), and enigmatic moments that you'll continue to discover wonderful facets of *A Christmas Tale* after multiple viewings. (You'll also find yourself changing your allegiances among these fascinatingly realistic characters, who are as compelling and infuriating as anyone you've ever known.) Critic Peter Travers perfectly summed up the film's appeal: "Holiday films in the hands of Hollywood make me puke. Mom is usually expiring from something terminal while the family dresses the Christmas tree with brave smiles. This French knockout, tough-minded and all the more affecting for it, turned my head around."

**FUN FACTS**

- Desplechin named Elisabeth's son "Paul Dedalus" not only as a reference to the mythological character whose son Icarus flew too close to the sun but also because it's the name of Amalric's character in the director's *My Sex Life . . . or How I Got into an Argument* (1996). "A way to say," per Desplechin, "I've already filmed your future. You're having a hard time now, but one day you will have a life."

- Desplechin cited an odd mix of holiday films as his influences: *Fanny and Alexander* (p. 35), *The Dead* (see below), *Home for the Holidays* (1995), *The Myth of Fingerprints* (1997), *What's Cooking?* (2000), and *The Royal Tenenbaums* (2001). Regarding the latter, journalist Dennis Lim noted that while it isn't a holiday film per se, it is "a family drama about the allure and danger of a family myth."

- Deneuve plays Mastroianni's mother-in-law in *A Christmas Tale*, but off screen they are mother and daughter.

- The Criterion DVD includes *L'aimée* (2007), a short film that inspired Desplechin to make this feature; he and his father go through their home at Roubaix looking at pictures and remembering old stories as they prepare to sell the family house.

# *The Dead* (1987)

PG; 83 min. Written by Tony Huston, based on the story "The Dead" from the collection *Dubliners* by James Joyce. Directed by John Huston. Starring Angelica Huston, Donal McCann, Dan O'Herlihy, Donal Donnelly. (Lionsgate Home Video)

In 1904 Dublin, the Morkan sisters host their annual dinner celebrating the 12th day of Christmas—January 6, the Feast of the Epiphany. Food is served, port is poured, songs are sung, and at least one of the gentlemen has a little too much to drink. As Gabriel Conroy

(McCann), nephew of the hostesses, is leaving with his wife Gretta (Angelica Huston), famed tenor Bartell D'Arcy (Frank Patterson) is finally prevailed upon to sing. His choice of tune stops Gretta in her tracks on the staircase. Later, she tearfully confesses to her husband that the song was one that a young boy who once loved her used to sing to her; he later died of consumption after spending the rainy night before Gretta left for convent school standing outside her window. Gabriel realizes there are facets of his wife's life that he never knew, but the revelation makes him love her—and life itself—all the more.

James Joyce's "The Dead" is considered by many to be one of the greatest short stories in the English language, but so very little actually happens in the tale that it presented a challenge to any filmmaker who might have considered adapting it to the big screen. You'd never know that, though, after watching the final film made by the legendary John Huston, who takes the depth of feeling and emotional impact of Joyce's story and makes it a haunting and riveting movie. Huston's camera dwells on the details of the dinner, but everything in the film winds up being a prelude to Gretta sharing her memories with her husband, and to Gabriel's understanding of these revelations. (Huston and McCann's performances couldn't be better; unplug the phone and drink in the power of their scenes together.) Christmas movies are often about families dealing with secrets of the past, and *The Dead* brilliantly examines the reverberations that early events from our lives have on our later days.

**FUN FACTS**
- John Huston was 80 years old during the making of the film; connected to oxygen tubes and confined to a wheelchair after battles with emphysema and heart disease, he watched the filming through a monitor and spoke to the crew via microphone. Filming lasted from January through April 1987; he died in August of that year, and the film was released posthumously. His daughter

Angelica starred, and his son Tony wrote the screenplay and served as his father's assistant on the set.

- Apart from a few exterior shots, the entire film was shot in a warehouse in Valencia, Calif.; the final shot of snow falling was filmed at Joshua Tree National Park in Twentynine Palms, Calif.
- Beware of a DVD version that was released by Lionsgate in 2009 that's missing an entire reel (10 minutes) of the film; the company recalled the discs, but make sure you don't pick up that 73-minute version by mistake.

## *Eyes Wide Shut* (1999)

R; 159 min. Written by Frederic Raphael and Stanley Kubrick, based on Arthur Schnitzler's *Traumnovelle*. Directed by Stanley Kubrick. Starring Tom Cruise, Nicole Kidman, Sydney Pollack, Todd Field. (Warner Home Video)

At a Christmas party, Manhattan physician Bill Harford (Cruise) and his wife Alice (Kidman) are sexually propositioned, separately; she turns down her suitor because she's married, but he seems to send his away only because he is called into service when the mistress of the party's host (Pollack) overdoses in the bathroom. The following night, Bill and Alice smoke pot and ask each other what transpired at the party. They argue over whether or not men and women think about sex differently, and Alice admits that, years earlier, she saw a Naval officer when she and Bill were vacationing in Cape Cod. If the officer had wanted to, she would have thrown away her family just to make love with him one time; not having done so, however, made Bill dearer to her than ever before. This revelation sets Bill off on a tour of New York's sexual underground, from a chat with a prostitute (Vinessa Shaw) to an encounter with an erotically precocious young girl (Leelee Sobieski) to a mysterious orgy outside of town.

Stanley Kubrick's final film is most often remembered for pairing the then-espoused Cruise and Kidman in a movie that addressed strong sexual themes in the context of marriage, but Christmas weaves its way through the film from start to finish, as does a murder mystery that might or might not involve the woman whose life Bill saves at the party. Kubrick underlines his protagonist's ambivalence about marriage, home, and family by unspooling this tale in a season of familial warmth and closeness. There's a perverse sense of humor about the movie—on the night after the party, Bill finds sexual opportunity around every corner, but when he goes out again actively looking for it, all doors slam in his face. Since Kubrick preferred to shoot everything in England, there's a certain fakiness to his Manhattan—it's certainly not as lavishly lit as the real thing is around the holidays—but *Eyes Wide Shut* is nonetheless a provocative movie that seems, like many of Kubrick's films, to get better with each passing year.

**FUN FACTS**
- Raphael also wrote *Two for the Road* (1967), another movie about a young married couple at a crossroads and dealing with each other's sexual past and unrequited desires. Raphael had to fight to get screen credit after Kubrick tried to claim sole credit for the screenplay.
- The orgy password, "*Fidelio*," is a reference to Beethoven's opera about a woman who disguises herself as a prison guard to save her husband's life.
- Kubrick was said to have considered Steve Martin for the lead role.
- Jocelyn Pook, once a member of the British pop group The Communards, composed the odd music played during the orgy sequence. The piece includes a Romanian orthodox Divine Liturgy played backwards.
- Kubrick includes several self-referential moments in the film: a sign reads "Bowman" and one of Bill's patients is named

"Kaminsky," which were the names of two of the astronauts in *2001: A Space Odyssey* (1968); a VHS cassette of *Full Metal Jacket* (1987) is visible in Bill's apartment; the mask Bill wears to the orgy is modeled from the face of Ryan O'Neal, star of *Barry Lyndon* (1975); *Blume in Love* (1973)—directed by Paul Mazursky, who made his acting debut in Kubrick's *Fear and Desire* (1953)—airs on a TV set.

- *Eyes Wide Shut* is generally considered to be the longest continuous shoot in film history; Cruise and Kidman signed contracts tying them to the production for as long as Kubrick needed them, but Harvey Keitel and Jennifer Jason Leigh both dropped out due to commitments to other films. They were later replaced by Pollack and Marie Richardson.

- For the film's U.S. release, Kubrick had to digitally cover up some naked bodies in the orgy sequence to get an "R" rating. The uncut version that the rest of the world got to see has subsequently made it onto DVD.

## Fanny and Alexander (Fanny och Alexander) (1982)

R; 188 min. (theatrical version)/312 min. (mini-series version). Written and directed by Ingmar Bergman. Starring Bertil Guve, Pernilla Allwin, Ewa Fröling, Erland Josephson. (The Criterion Collection)

The Ekdahl family gathers for its annual Christmas celebration; before everyone comes to the home of matriarch Helena (Gunn Wållgren), theater owner Oscar (Allan Edwall) and his family perform the annual Christmas play, restaurateur Gustav Adolf (Jarl Kulle) hosts a lavish party for the cast and crew, and unhappy academic Carl (Börge Ahlstedt) drinks and argues with his German wife Lydia (Christina Schollin). Their Christmas is grand and glorious, but not long after, Oscar dies of a heart attack. His wife Emilie (Fröling) marries the stern and cruel Bishop Edvard Vergerus (Jan Malmsjö); can the Ekdahls, with the help of Helena's old lover Isak (Joseph-son), rescue Emilie and her children Fanny (Allwin) and Alexander (Guve) from this monstrous new household?

Ingmar Bergman has a reputation for being a cold, depressing, ascetic filmmaker, but *Fanny and Alexander* brims over with a love for living, for family, and for filmmaking itself. The 188-minute ver-sion of the film, released theatrically in most of the world, opens with a lovely Christmas sequence, but the activities of December 24 take up the entire first chapter of the original mini-series that Berg-man created for Danish television. As dish after dish is served and presents are opened, we get to know the entire Ekdahl clan and its relationships with each other and with its household staff. (Frisky Gustav Adolf is always chasing a chambermaid, while other servants find it a shocking breach of decorum that Helena insists that the staff eat Christmas dinner at the same huge table with the family.) The opening act of *Fanny and Alexander* is as perfect an evocation of the sensual delights of Christmas as has ever been captured on film— you'll find memories of the film figuring into your nostalgic holiday yearnings.

**FUN FACTS**
- The mini-series version of the Ekdahl Christmas features several segments cut out for the shorter film version, including Alexan-der's vision of death in the living room, Helena's walk through the house before the party, the shots of the audience (which includes Bishop Vergerus) before the play begins, the entire dinner se-quence, and Oscar's nursery story about the most valuable chair in the world. The argument between Carl and Lydia, the breakfast scene, and the torch-lighting and sleigh ride scene all run shorter as well.
- The film won four Academy Awards: Best Foreign Film, Best Cin-ematography, Best Costume Design, and Best Art Decoration-Set

Decoration; Bergman was nominated for Best Director and Best Screenplay.

- Keep an eye peeled for future film star Lena Olin (1988's *The Unbearable Lightness of Being*) as one of the maids in the Ekdahl house.

## *Female Trouble* (1974)

**R; 89 min. Written and directed by John Waters. Starring Divine, David Lochary, Mink Stole, Edith Massey. (New Line Home Entertainment)**

High school dropout Dawn Davenport (Divine) runs away from home on Christmas Day, but not before she upends the Christmas tree on her parents for their failure to buy her the cha-cha heels she wanted. Raped by the driver (also Divine) who picks her up, Dawn winds up giving birth to daughter Taffy, whom she continually mistreats. Dawn becomes a prostitute and thief alongside her high school friends, but is eventually "discovered" by beautician couple Donald (Lochary) and Donna Dasher (Mary Vivian Pearce). Operating under the theory that "Crime makes you more beautiful," the Dashers want to photograph Dawn while she commits illegal acts. Dawn marries beautician Gator (Michael Potter), much to the disgust of his aunt Ida (Massey), who disfigures Dawn by throwing acid in her face. The Dashers assure Dawn that the scars make her even more beautiful. Just before Dawn's big nightclub act, the now-grown Taffy (Stole) tells her mother that she has become a Hare Krishna. Dawn strangles the girl, then goes on stage and puts on a show that culminates with her shooting at the audience. The Dashers betray Dawn at her trial, but she's thrilled at all the publicity she's getting from the tabloid press after being condemned to die in the electric chair.

Say what you want about John Waters and his outrageously tasteless sense of humor—he's all about the holidays. In fact, if you haven't already read his essay, "Why I Love Christmas," from the collection *Crackpot: The Obsessions of John Waters*, go get it right now and make it part of your annual festivities. One of the highlights of the piece is his childhood reminiscence about arriving at Grandma's house with his parents to discover that the tree had fallen over and pinned the old lady under it—Waters pinpoints that memory as the inspiration for the famous early sequence of *Female Trouble* when Dawn attacks her folks with the tannenbaum. Christmas occupies just the first few minutes of this cult classic, but it's such an indelible, signature moment that the film definitely ranks as a holiday must.

**FUN FACTS**

- The electric chair where Dawn meets her fate became a cherished prop for writer-director Waters, who still displays it in his home.
- The jurors at Divine's trial are all played by parents and other relatives of cast and crew members.
- Divine performed his own stunts in the film; he trained at a YMCA to get his trampoline flips down.
- Waters says his working title for the film was *Rotten Mind, Rotten Face*.

## *Less than Zero* (1987)

**R; 98 min. Written by Harley Peyton, based on the novel by Bret Easton Ellis. Directed by Marek Kanievska. Starring Andrew McCarthy, Robert Downey Jr., Jami Gertz, James Spader. (20th Century Fox Home Entertainment)**

Clay (McCarthy) returns to Los Angeles from his college back east for Christmas vacation. Over Thanksgiving, Clay was devastated to discover his girlfriend Blair (Gertz) had been sleeping with his life-long best friend Julian (Downey), but he tries putting all of that behind him and rebuilding his relationships with both of them. Julian, however, has sunk deeper and deeper into debt and drug addiction, to the point that he allows his dealer Rip (Spader) to pimp him out to male clients. Clay tries to save Julian and to convince Blair to leave Los Angeles with him but will find himself frustrated in both pursuits.

Ellis' 1985 novel because a cause célèbre at the time of its publication as a devastating portrait of nihilistic and hedonistic privileged youth in Los Angeles. By the time Hollywood was through with it, however, a story about rich teens who were blasé about drugs and alternative sexuality became an anti-drug screed that abhorred the possibility that Downey's character might be bisexual. (Movie-Clay is horrified to find Julian about to have sex with a man for drug money, while book-Clay is himself a bisexual cocaine user who blithely watches Julian commit that very act.) Not that there's anything wrong with cautionary tales about drug abuse, but that's the very last thing *Less than Zero* started out as. Still, the movie's worth a look for Downey and Spader's indelible performances, as well as for its glossy portrayal of an '80s Christmas among L.A.'s rich and doomed.

**FUN FACTS**
- Good luck spotting him, but a pre-fame Brad Pitt appears as an extra in the party scene where the fight breaks out; he was paid $38.
- Aljean Harmetz wrote a scathing piece for *The New York Times*, "Sanitizing a Novel for the Screen," about how the book's edgy content was "meetinged to death" by 20th Century Fox execs, who kept wanting to make the characters more likable and the story's moral more apparent. The studio hired Kanievska, according to Harmetz, "specifically because he had dealt with ambivalent sexuality and made unlikable characters appealing in *Another Country* [1984]."
- Despite his initial ambivalence about the film, Ellis has grown to appreciate it on its own terms. He has written a sequel to the novel, called *Imperial Bedrooms* (like *Less than Zero*, the title is

an Elvis Costello reference), and says he'd like to see the original cast reunited for a film version. McCarthy narrates the *Imperial Bedrooms* audiobook.

## *The Lion in Winter* (1968)

**PG; 134 min. Written by James Goldman, based on his play. Directed by Anthony Harvey. Starring Katharine Hepburn, Peter O'Toole, Anthony Hopkins, Timothy Dalton. (MGM Home Video)**

The year is 1183, and King Henry II (O'Toole) summons his wife Eleanor of Aquitaine (Hepburn) from the tower in which he has imprisoned her to stand by his side at a Christmas court at Chinon. The real occasion at hand is Henry's decision regarding which of his sons with Eleanor will inherit the throne after his death. Henry favors their somewhat dim youngest son, John (Nigel Terry), but Eleanor prefers accomplished warrior Richard the Lion-Hearted (Hopkins). Middle child Geoffrey (John Castle) is the most scheming yet the least appreciated by either parent. Adding to the palace intrigue is the arrival of France's King Philip (Dalton), son of Eleanor's ex-husband, brother to Henry's mistress—and himself a one-time lover of Richard's. And you thought *your* family holiday get-togethers were awkward and dysfunctional.

"Shall we hang the holly, or each other?" jokes Eleanor, and that pretty well sums up the dynamic here. Goldman, adapting his own play, takes British history and funnels it through *Who's Afraid of Virginia Woolf?* for this portrait of familial head games where real power, and life and death itself, are the stakes. O'Toole and Hepburn play their roles grandly, giving what were no doubt outsized characters in real life an indisputably immense presence on the screen. (What else is one to do with such overly theatrical dialogue as "Of course he has a knife, he always has a knife, we all have knives! It's 1183, and we're barbarians!"?) Patrick Stewart and Glenn Close tackled the lead roles for Andrei Konchalovsky's 2003 TV remake, but they never approach the larger-than-life glory of their predecessors.

**FUN FACTS**
- Peter O'Toole was twice Oscar-nominated for playing King Henry II, both here and in *Becket* (1964). Hepburn won her third Best Actress Oscar for this film, winding up in one of the Academy's rare ties (with Barbra Streisand for *Funny Girl*).
- *The Lion in Winter* was the first film for both Dalton and Hopkins. O'Toole was only 5, 7, and 13 years older, respectively, than Hopkins, Castle, and Terry but played their father nonetheless. Hepburn was 25 years older than O'Toole, although the real Eleanor was 11 years older than Henry.
- Historically speaking, there was no Christmas court at Chinon in 1183, although there was one at Caen in 1182.

## *Metropolitan* (1990)

PG-13; 98 min. Written and directed by Whit Stillman. Starring Chris Eigeman, Edward Clements, Carolyn Farina, Taylor Nichols. (The Criterion Collection)

College freshman Tom Townsend (Clements) doesn't think himself part of the upper-crusters that make up the Manhattan debutante ball scene every Christmas holiday, but he finds himself swept up into the "Sally Fowler Rat Pack" of rich preppy girls and their escorts. Guided by the cynical Nick (Eigeman), Tom soon becomes one of the gang that includes Audrey Rouget (Farina), a girl who has known and admired Tom for far longer than he realizes. Over the course of the school break, friendships will form and dissolve, debs will fall in and out of love, and these "UHBs" (urban haute bourgeoisie) will wonder if their whole way of life is about to come crashing to a halt.

Stillman's fiercely literate and articulate debut feature—how many other movies feature college students mixing it up over Fourier and Jane Austen between cocktails and conga lines?—is a whip-smart valentine to both the seriousness and callowness of young adults, to evening gowns and tuxedos, and to bright and funny repartée. None of the characters are quite what we think upon first viewing, and all of them are handled intelligently and lovingly by their creator. But *Metropolitan* is also a love letter to New York City at Christmastime, from the bustle of Rockefeller Center to the display windows on Fifth Avenue to midnight mass at St. Thomas Episcopal Church. Stillman hasn't been nearly as prolific as his fans would like—he's made only two more features since this extraordinary debut—but *Metropolitan* shows an auteur who's already in command of both his craft and the vagaries of the human heart.

**FUN FACTS**

- As an outtake on the Criterion Collection DVD shows, actor Will Kempe—eventually cast as the dastardly Rick Von Sloneker—was originally set to play Nick.
- The character of Audrey (once again played by Farina) turns up in Stillman's *The Last Days of Disco* (1998), where a character refers to her as a major player in New York City publishing. All those arguments with Tom over *Mansfield Park* must have paid off.
- Stillman intentionally never reveals whether the movie is period or contemporary. Since the costumes are all safely conservative and preppy, and since the characters vaguely lament that this may be the last year of deb balls "because of everything that's going on," only the late, lamented Checker Cabs—and, years after the film's release, the fact that *Metropolitan* takes place before *The Last Days of Disco*—give the film any specific grounding in time.
- Not only did the production have the good fortune to film the last of the legendary Christmas windows of the historic Scribner's

bookstore, but they also lucked out in that it was a display of Jane Austen novels.

- Stillman: "Rather than make the usual grainy film on some gritty subject, my idea was to photograph the most elegant Manhattan story possible. New York is at its most beautiful between Thanksgiving and Christmastime, and for next to no cost we had a set worth billions."

## A Midnight Clear (1992)

R; 107 min. Written by Keith Gordon, based on the novel by William Wharton. Directed by Keith Gordon. Starring Ethan Hawke, Gary Sinise, Peter Berg, Arye Gross, Kevin Dillon, Frank Whaley. (Sony Pictures Home Entertainment)

It's mid-December 1944, and soldier Will Knott (Hawke)—known as "Won't" to the rest of his squad—observes commanding officer "Mother" (Sinise) having a breakdown, stripping off his clothes and jumping into an icy stream in the Ardennes Forest after receiving news that his baby has died. Will doesn't report the incident, and their intelligence squad—made up of soldiers who got high scores on intelligence tests—are sent out on another assignment, occupying a house near two roads where another company has disappeared. The soldiers find a squadron of Nazis nearby, but it soon becomes apparent—particularly when the enemy soldiers stand outside near the house and sing Christmas carols in German and Latin—that the Germans want to surrender to the Americans rather than get sent to the Russian front. The Americans and the Germans agree to stage a fake skirmish right after Christmas, after which the Americans will "capture" the opposing combatants, but wartime can make even the best-laid plans go awry.

Whether they are set among the military (1996's *Mother Night*) or in a prep school (1988's *The Chocolate War*), many of actor-turned-director Keith Gordon's films are literary adaptations dealing with men struggling against authoritarian power structures. *A Midnight Clear* definitely fits this category, and it's a gut-punchingly powerful movie that benefits from an extraordinary ensemble of actors. From the haunting flashback of four virgin soldiers looking for a woman to relieve them of their burden before they ship out to the tragic realism of the battle sequences, this is a movie that doesn't in the least glamorize war or its effect on the poor, brave souls called upon to fight.

**FUN FACTS**
- Five of the six leads—Hawke, Sinise, Peter Berg, Arye Gross, and Frank Whaley—followed Gordon's lead and went on to direct feature films themselves.
- While set near the French-German border, *A Midnight Clear* was actually shot in Utah, during what turned out to be the coldest winter in 83 years. The house's interior was built inside a high school gymnasium, with the attic set constructed in the same school's theater.

## *My Night at Maud's (Ma nuit chez Maud)* (1969)

Unrated; 111 min. Written and directed by Eric Rohmer. Starring Jean-Louis Trintignant, Françoise Fabian, Marie-Christine Barrault. (The Criterion Collection)

Intellectual Jean-Louis (Trintignant) becomes smitten with Françoise (Barrault), a young woman he sees at church. A strict Catholic, Jean-Louis nonetheless finds himself consumed with philosophical issues, particularly the writings of Pascal. His friend Vidal (Antoine Vitez) invites him to meet Maud, a divorced woman he knows, and the two men visit her after Midnight Mass on Christmas Eve. The three of them discuss randomness, probability, sex. Vidal leaves, and Jean-Louis and Maud continue talking. Jean-Louis eventually spends a chaste night in her bed, and while there's some awkwardness in the morning—he attempts to break his vow not to have sex with Maud, but she rebuffs him—she still invites him to a trip to the mountains that day. On his way home from Maud's apartment, he runs into Françoise and attempts to initiate conversation with her. Jean-Louis finds himself torn between two beautiful women—a fellow Catholic and a free-thinker.

Nobody makes a dialogue-packed movie as riveting as Rohmer, and one of his masterpieces would have to be this exploration of relationships, personal morality, and sexual ethics that's the centerpiece of his "Six Moral Tales" series. Christmas figures into the film in interesting ways, not only to highlight Jean-Louis and Françoise's Catholic beliefs but also for a lovely scene in which—after Jean-Louis, Vidal, and Maud have spent half the night having a heady conversation about philosophy—Maud's young daughter enters, wanting nothing more than to stare at the lights on the Christmas tree. It's the divide between the characters' ethics and their actions—what they say and what they do—that makes the film so fascinating.

See also: Rohmer's *Tale of Winter* (1992), one of his "Tales of the Four Seasons," is also set at Christmas and also deals with a love triangle—in this case, however, it's a woman torn between two men who are each convenient for her in their own way, while she really pines for the man she met on vacation years earlier with whom she has lost touch.

**FUN FACTS**

- Rohmer's real name is Maurice Henri Joseph Schérer—he created his pen name by taking "Eric" from director Erich von Stroheim and "Rohmer" from Sax Rohmer, creator of Fu Manchu. Before he became a filmmaker, Rohmer was an editor of the French film journal *Cahiers du cinéma*; like many of his peers at the magazine,

Rohmer went on to become one of the key filmmakers of the French New Wave of the 1960s.

- The "Six Moral Tales" all loosely follow the basic plot of F. W. Murnau's silent classic *Sunrise* (1927)—a man, either married or otherwise committed to one woman, is tempted by a second woman. *My Night at Maud's* was Rohmer's first international hit.

- *My Night at Maud's* is one of the rare films to be nominated for an Oscar in two separate years—it was up for Best Foreign Film in 1970 and Best Original Screenplay in 1971. (Academy rules have since been changed to prevent eligibility in more than one year.)

## *The Ref* (1994)

**R; 93 min. Written by Richard LaGravenese and Marie Weiss. Directed by Ted Demme. Starring Denis Leary, Judy Davis, Kevin Spacey. (Buena Vista Home Entertainment)**

Perpetually bickering couple Caroline (Davis) and Lloyd (Spacey) don't let the holidays get in the way of their constant verbal warfare. Unlucky jewel thief Gus (Leary) takes the couple hostage when a Christmas Eve burglary goes awry, and if he wants to elude the police, he's going to have to play marriage counselor to force these two to get along. Gus' attempts to keep the peace are threatened by the appearance of Lloyd's harpy of a mother (Glynis Johns) and dull brother Gary (Adam LeFevre), Gary's shrewish wife Connie (Christine Baranski), and Lloyd and Caroline's juvenile delinquent son Jesse (Robert J. Steinmiller Jr.). Can Gus figure out a way to elude the oafish local cops and get out of town before this family drives him up the wall?

If you're looking for actors who can do caustic, Davis, Spacey, and Leary more than fill the bill, and they're completely in step with the corrosively funny script of *The Ref.* Tolstoy famously noted that all unhappy families are unhappy in their own way, and this comedy was one of the first American movies to acknowledge that unhappy families are perhaps at their unhappiest at Christmastime. And while the movie gets disappointingly soft in its final scenes, the wickedly funny barbs that the cast tosses at one another make *The Ref* a must-see for fans of deliciously sour laughs.

**FUN FACTS**

- The character played by J. K. Simmons, a military school commander being blackmailed by Jesse, is named "Siskel," a way for LaGravenese to get revenge on film critic Gene Siskel, who had panned one of the screenwriter's earlier films.
- *The Ref* was a rare comedy to be executive-produced by action-meisters Don Simpson and Jerry Bruckheimer. It was also one of their few flops, grossing only $11.5 million in the U.S. (The fact that this Christmas-set comedy was released in March probably didn't help.)
- Glynis Johns refused to use a stunt double and actually elbowed Leary in the stomach and groin in their fight scene.
- The billiard ball eaten by the guard dog, according to the American Humane Association, was made of dog food and coated with an edible glaze similar to that used in making gingerbread houses.
- The production went through 450 candles shooting the Scandinavian dinner scene, which features the lead characters wearing blazing wreaths on their heads.

## *Some Girls* (1988)

R; 94 min. Written by Rupert Walters. Directed by Michael Hoffman. Starring Patrick Dempsey, Jennifer Connelly, Lila Kedrova, André Gregory. (MGM Home Entertainment)

Cocky college student Michael (Dempsey) travels to Québec City to spend Christmas with his girlfriend Gaby (Connelly), who has been out of school because of her grandmother's illness. Upon his arrival, Gaby informs Michael that she no longer loves him, but that's just the first of many shocks to his system. At her family's sprawling house, Michael meets Gaby's flirtatious sisters Irenka (Sheila Kelley) and Simone (Ashley Greenfield); her father (Gregory), an academic who can work only in the nude—and who, like the hero of *My Night at Maud's* (p. 44), is obsessed with Pascal; and her strictly Catholic, no-nonsense mother (Florinda Bolkan), who immediately treats Michael like a fox in the henhouse. At the hospital, Gaby's sick grandmother (Kedrova) mistakes Michael for another Michael—her late husband. And so goes an unforgettable Christmas over which Michael will discover that, like all men, he will never truly understand anything about the mysteries of women.

Even with all the cards stacked against Michael Hoffman's charming romantic comedy—MGM suffered one of its many bankruptcies around the time of the film's meager, underpublicized release—*Some Girls* has gone on to earn a cult following on DVD and cable. Sporting the kind of breezy boldness we're used to seeing only in European sex comedies, this sprightly farce is urbane, smart, and sensual. It also doesn't hurt that the cast is so sparkling, from Dempsey and Connelly (whose careers would later explode on TV and in film, respectively) to old troopers like Kedrova, Bolkan, and Gregory. The subtlety and intelligence of Walters' delightful screenplay reward multiple viewings, and the visuals of snowy Québec City at Christmas time (shot by cinematographer Ueli Steiger) will make you want to plan your next holiday there.

**FUN FACTS**

- *Some Girls* was one of the first screenplays to be developed through the Sundance Institute; Robert Redford is credited as an executive producer.
- The mural being hung on the walls while Michael waits at the airport is a reproduction of the Three Graces from Botticelli's "Primavera," a visual metaphor for the three sisters who will bewitch Michael during his visit.

## *The Store* (1983)

**Unrated; 118 min. Directed by Frederick Wiseman. (Zipporah Films)**

Documentary filmmaker Frederick Wiseman brings his camera to downtown Dallas, recording the goings-on at Neiman-Marcus' flagship department store during the Christmas shopping season. We eavesdrop on meetings with department heads —"One word, the reason for it all—sales."—and calisthenic sessions with cashiers who exercise their fingers (for button-pushing on the cash registers) and their faces (for all the smiling they're going to be doing). Jewelry gets designed, created, and sold. Employees dressed as elves randomly wander the store as woodwind quartets and children's choirs perform Christmas carols. (At one point, even a customer gets into the spirit and belts out a few tunes himself.) It's a fascinating portrait of what goes into the buying and the selling during the busiest retail season of the year.

Wiseman has correctly stated that there's no such thing as unbiased documentary filmmaking, but he definitely goes out of his way not to guide the audience. There's no narrator, no score, not even interviews—he just stands back and shoots while salesmen talk up the virtues of wild Russian sable or diamond settings, secretaries get singing telegrams, customers pose for photo portraits, and division heads discuss matters that include everything from food placement in the epicurean section to the whereabouts of a missing chandelier. There's a brand of exuberant extravagance that's unique to Dallas, and *The Store*—filmed in November and December of 1982—revels in the *Dynasty*-era glory of chunky jewelry, big hair and shoulder pads, Bill Blass fashion shows, and tables loaded with stuffed E.T. dolls. (It's a movie that would make a perfect double-bill with David Byrne's *True Stories* (1986) or Robert Altman's *Dr. T and the Women* (2000), two other films that at least indirectly deal with conspicuous consumption, Texas-style.) Shopping has become one of the integral facets of the Christmas experience, and this documentary walks us through the showrooms and the meeting rooms where merchants decide what we're going to buy.

**FUN FACTS**

- While Wiseman's earlier documentaries dealt with grittier subject matter—titles include *Hospital* (1970) and *Juvenile Court* (1973)—the director insisted upon completion of *The Store* that the film fit perfectly into what he called his "institutional series" of movies about places that are common experiences in people's lives. He told *The New York Times,* "If you are going to have theories about American society, you've got to look at all aspects of it. You've got to look at how the images are created that affect people's lives and the choices of consumer goods they buy."

- *The Store* was shot over four weeks between Thanksgiving and Christmas 1982—the crew was given free rein over the store— and was funded by Wiseman's MacArthur Foundation "genius grant"; New York's PBS station turned down his grant application, asking him why he had selected Neiman-Marcus in Texas rather than Manhattan's Macy's or Gimbels. The Corporation for Public Broadcasting eventually overruled the previous panel and partially funded the film after shooting was completed.

- This was the first documentary that Wiseman shot in color.

## Venus Beauty Institute (*Vénus beauté [institut]*) (1999)

R; 105 min. Written by Tonie Marshall, Jacques Audiard, and Marion Vernoux. Directed by Tonie Marshall. Starring Nathalie Baye, Bulle Ogier, Mathilde Seigner, Audrey Tautou. (Fox Lorber Home Video)

Paris is covered in Christmas decorations, but the season isn't bringing much joy to Angèle (Baye), a 40-year-old aesthetician at the Venus Beauty salon. She just wants to find a man who will take her to the movies and take her to bed; instead, she gets Antoine (Samuel Le Bihan), a shaggy-haired, bearded man who watches her get dumped at a train station and is immediately smitten. Despite having a fiancée, Antoine courts Angèle, who thinks that "love is a form of slavery" and that it makes her "sick and mean." Meanwhile, Angèle's coworker Marie (Tautou) is being wooed herself, by a much older widower who becomes enchanted with her over the course of his weekly facials.

The French are masters at stories about romantic disappointment, and the ups and downs of *l'amour fou* are the stuff of high comedy in this charming import. Baye, one of the great leading ladies of Gallic cinema, is thoroughly believable as a beautiful woman who has avoided love and commitment but realizes that the time may be coming for her to put away girlish things. The movie is also a great workplace comedy, wringing laughs out of the salon's oddball clients (the lady who gets made up for outlandish costume parties as well as her opposite, a tanning-addicted woman who doesn't care who sees her naked) and from uptight boss Nadine, played to well-coiffed perfection by Ogier.

**FUN FACTS**

- The Internet Movie Database plot keywords for the film include "Christmas," "Mad Love" and "Electrolysis."
- Years before she would star in *Amélie* (2001) or become the face of Chanel, Tautou was honored with a César Award for Most Promising Actress for her role in *Venus Beauty Institute*. The film also won awards for Best Picture, Best Director, and Best Screenplay.
- Director Tonie Marshall's father is American actor William Marshall, a 1940s film star whose credits include *Knute Rockne, All American* (1940), *Santa Fe Trail* (1940), and the original *State Fair* (1945).

(left to right) David Ogden Stiers, Kim Darby, John Cusack, and Scooter
Stevens in *Better Off Dead* (1985).

# Like a Bowlful of Jelly
## CHRISTMAS COMEDIES

Christmas can make you crazy if you let it—everyone's so busy with social engagements, decorating, buying and wrapping presents, and sending Christmas cards that it's a wonder that more of us don't snap from the stress. Every so often, you just have to stop and laugh at it all.

And besides, aren't some of your favorite Christmas memories the funny ones? Putting gift bows on the dog, recalling elaborate delicacies that didn't make it out of the oven, or swapping stories about the worst gifts ever are always good for some chuckles. (Somewhere in the stacks of my family's slide carousels is a beloved photo combining two terrible gifts we received one year—my brothers and I are holding our noses as we dangle 100% acrylic sweaters over a padded toilet seat.) So don't let the holidays, and that blustery cold-and-flu-season weather, get you down. Give your immune system a break and have some laughs with these hilarious Christmas comedies.

## *About a Boy* (2002)

PG-13; 101 min. Written by Peter Hedges, Chris Weitz, and Paul Weitz, based on the novel by Nick Hornby. Directed by Chris and Paul Weitz. Starring Hugh Grant, Nicholas Hoult, Toni Collette, Rachel Weisz. (Universal Home Entertainment)

Will (Grant) has made a lifestyle out of being unemployed and un-committed. He lives comfortably off the royalties of "Santa's Super Sleigh," a ridiculous Christmas carol written by his father—it's not unlike the awful but earworm-y "Hooray for Santa Claus" from *Santa Claus Conquers the Martians* (p. 184)—and he breezily avoids getting tied down to the women who drift in and out of his stunning but sterile bachelor digs. At one point, Will figures that single moms make the perfect conquests; he comes off better than whatever jerk just dumped her, and then she'll eventually drop him because she's not ready to have a man in her life. But then he meets the unstable Fiona (Collette) and her shy, nerdy son Marcus (Hoult) and finds himself actually having to be there for another human being. Is Will ready to leave his old life behind and actually start believing that "no man is an island"?

This sweetly warm and witty adaptation of the wonderful Nick Hornby novel features a passel of terrific performances—Grant has perhaps never been better at playing a shallow cad—and the two Christmas sequences tie the overall plot together perfectly. Even with American screenwriters and directors, this movie feels essentially British, but at the same time, its characters and situations are so recognizable as to be utterly universal. And who would have guessed that Hoult would transform from the awk-ward tween of this movie to playing much more adult objects of desire on the BBC series *Skins* and in Tom Ford's *A Single Man* (2009)?

**FUN FACTS**

- The Weitz brothers are third-generation Hollywood; their grandparents are Mexican screen legend Lupita Tovar and studio-exec-turned-agent Paul Kohner (the couple met when she came to Hollywood to star in the Spanish-language *Dracula* in 1931); their uncle is director-producer Pancho Kohner; their parents are actress Susan Kohner, an Oscar nominee for the remake of *Imitation of Life* (1959), and fashion designer John Weitz.

- Co-writer Peter Hedges must have a thing for holidays—his directorial debut, *Pieces of April* (2003), takes place entirely on Thanksgiving.

- The film's delightful song score was composed and performed by Damon Gough, under his stage name, Badly Drawn Boy. While not Christmas music, it's nonetheless a great soundtrack.

- Will's reference to Haley Joel Osment is something of an inside joke, since Collette played Osment's mother in *The Sixth Sense* (1999).

## Better Off Dead (1985)

PG; 97 min. Written and directed by Savage Steve Holland. Starring John Cusack, Diane Franklin, David Ogden Stiers, Kim Darby. (Paramount Home Video)

When Lane Meyer (Cusack) gets dumped by the object of his obsession—girlfriend Beth (Amanda Wyss)—suicide seems like the only option, but his attempts at it all go grandly wrong. Failing to do himself in, Lane decides he'll win her back by skiing the infamous K-12 slope, which has been conquered by just one person: Beth's new boyfriend, the arrogant and obnoxious Roy Stalin (Aaron Dozier). If Lane manages to ski the K-12 without breaking his neck, maybe he'll figure out that the real girl of his dreams is Monique (Franklin), the French exchange student staying with the weird Smith family across the street.

There's not a whole lot of plot in Holland's feature debut, but what makes *Better Off Dead* such a cult favorite is its wall-to-wall absurdist humor, from the ubiquitous paperboy who chases Lane through town demanding "MY TWO DOLLARS!" to the horrifying food prepared by Lane's mom (Darby) to the girl who's dating the entire basketball team to the claymation hamburger that channels Van Halen. One of the movie's most quoted lines comes when the obnoxious Mrs. Smith (Laura Waterbury) tells Monique, "That's a Christmas present. Do you have Christmas in France?" Then she squeezes the girl's cheeks and screeches, "Chriiiist-maaas. *CHRIIIIST-MAAASSSS!*"

### FUN FACTS

- The Korean drag racer who impersonates Howard Cosell was dubbed by impressionist Rich Little.
- A character standing behind Beth at the New Year's dance is wearing a striped "Freddy Krueger" sweater—actress Wyss portrayed Krueger's first victim in the horror hit *A Nightmare on Elm Street* (1984).
- Actor Dan Schneider—who would go on to star in TV's *Head of the Class* before becoming a successful producer of children's television—later noted that he completely improvised Ricky Smith's dorky dance moves.
- Two interesting tidbits from an interview with Holland: The girl who broke his heart in real life called him and said, "I've been in therapy because I saw your movie, and I had no idea." Holland also reveals that Cusack hated the movie. The director screened *Better Off Dead* on the set of his follow-up film *One Crazy Summer* (1986), which also starred Cusack, and Holland claims Cusack came up to him afterwards and said, "You know, you tricked me. *Better Off Dead* was the worst thing I have ever

seen. I will never trust you as a director ever again, so don't speak to me."

## Christmas in Connecticut (1945)

Unrated; 102 min. Written by Lionel Houser and Adele Comandini; story by Aileen Hamilton. Directed by Peter Godfrey. Starring Barbara Stanwyck, Dennis Morgan, Sydney Greenstreet, S. Z. Sakall. (Warner Home Video)

Magazine readers coast to coast swear by the homemaking advice of Elizabeth Lane (Stanwyck), who writes about cooking, cleaning, and handicrafts from the beautiful Connecticut estate she shares with her husband and child. What her many fans don't know is that she's a fraud—Elizabeth is unmarried and childless, lives in an apartment in Manhattan, and relies on Felix (Sakall), who owns the restaurant downstairs, to do all her cooking. When war hero Jefferson Jones (Morgan) writes a fan letter to her magazine—he reads her columns while recovering in the hospital (where he's denied solid food)—publisher Alexander Yardley (Greenstreet) decides it would be a publicity coup to have Jones spend Christmas with Elizabeth and her family. To keep her job, Elizabeth's going to have to come up with a fake house, husband, and child—and if that weren't tricky enough, the "married" writer finds herself falling in love with her fan.

Decades before Martha Stewart made us feel inadequate in the kitchen, there were plenty of experts writing about whipping together soufflé for breakfast before building your very own log cabin in the afternoon. So it's something of a relief to find out that, just maybe, some of these home-ec whizzes are really faking it. Stanwyck and Morgan (who looks a lot like *Glee* star Matthew Morrison) have real chemistry, and Greenstreet and Sakall—who both appeared in *Casablanca* (1941)—rank among Hollywood's greatest scene-stealing second bananas. And it definitely says something about America in 1945 that you could open a breezy romantic comedy with a scene of a U.S. troop ship getting sunk by a U-boat (Jones is one of two survivors).

**FUN FACTS**

- Arnold Schwarzenegger made his directorial debut with a 1992 made-for-TV remake starring Dyan Cannon and Kris Kristofferson. Suffice it to say that it's no mystery why the governor of California was never asked to direct again.
- If the Connecticut farmhouse looks familiar, it's because the set was also used in *Bringing Up Baby* (1938).
- Like many films that now pop up on TV every December as holiday favorites, *Christmas in Connecticut* wasn't originally released at the end of the year—it opened on August 11, 1945. The film has come to be considered a classic over the years, but Time magazine's critic at the time called it "thoroughly moth-eaten."
- Sakall, famous for his kind, jowly face, was often credited in films as S. Z. "Cuddles" Sakall, although he apparently hated the nickname.
- In 2007, *Variety* announced that another remake of *Christmas in Connecticut* would go into production.

## *Comfort and Joy* (1984)

PG; 106 min. Written and directed by Bill Forsyth. Starring Bill Paterson, Eleanor David, Clare Grogan. (Currently not available on DVD in the U.S.)

Radio DJ Alan "Dickie" Bird (Paterson) is devastated when, just before Christmas, his beloved girlfriend Maddy (David) walks out on him. (He keeps dreaming of her return, making him all the more depressed when he wakes up alone.) Alan's life seems to be going nowhere, until he finds himself caught between two rival gangs of ice-cream truck operators. (When Alan starts using his radio show to pass messages between "Mr. Bunny" and "Mr. McCool," the station manager begins to think Alan is nuts, prompting the boss to ask his lawyer, "Do you think there's a sanity clause?") Can Alan use the popular "Dickie Bird" radio show to bring an end to this frozen-treat gang warfare in Glasgow? And will brokering a truce help him to finally get on with his life?

Writer-director Bill Forsyth, at his peak, was one of the great observers of everyday comedy and tragedy. With international favorites like *Gregory's Girl* (1981) and *Local Hero* (1983), he hit on a perfect formula that involved recognizably human eccentricity, subtle and deadpan wit, and the universal search for love and understanding. One of his best films, *Comfort and Joy* gives us a bleak and rainy Scotland that's nonetheless suffused with the Christmas spirit, with soggy Santas everywhere. Dickie Bird may feel rejected and alone, but everyone—including the ice-cream thugs who keep destroying his car—asks him for an autograph and to make a request on his popular morning show. Balancing laughs, sweetness, and an underlying tone of melancholy, Forsyth concocted one of the all-time great Christmas movies. Here's hoping a U.S. video company finally gives this delightful movie the domestic DVD release it so richly deserves.

**FUN FACTS**
- There was a real "Ice Cream War" in early-1980s Glasgow that inspired this film; it was later suspected that drug dealers, using ice-cream trucks to hide their business, were battling over turf. The subsequent court cases of those arrested for murder in the fracas dragged on for 20 years.
- At a 2001 screening, Forsyth said he removed a scene toward the end of the film that implied the possibility of a romance between Alan and Charlotte (Clare Grogan), the girl from the ice-cream van. Grogan, who also appeared in Forsyth's *Gregory's Girl*, is

perhaps best known as the lead singer for Scottish New Wave band Altered Images.

- Forsyth claimed that a major inspiration for his screenplay was the Dire Straits album *Love Over Gold*, so it's no wonder that several lines of dialogue paraphrase lyrics by the band. Forsyth also hired Dire Straits frontman Mark Knopfler to compose the score.
- *Comfort and Joy* was the film selected for the first-ever royal premiere held in Los Angeles, in honor of Britain's Princess Anne in July of 1984.

## Desk Set (1957)

Unrated; 103 min. Written by Phoebe and Henry Ephron, based on the play by William Marchant. Directed by Walter Lang. Starring Spencer Tracy, Katharine Hepburn, Joan Blondell, Gig Young. (20th Century Fox Home Entertainment)

When efficiency expert Richard Sumner (Tracy) starts sniffing around the research department of the Federal Broadcasting Company TV network, the librarians naturally get suspicious. That department's head, Bunny Watson (Hepburn), knows that Sumner is the inventor of an "electronic brain" called EMERAC, and she worries that if he installs one of his supercomputers, she and research librarians Peg (Blondell), Sylvia (Dina Merrill), and Ruthie (Sue Randall) will all be out of a job. The more time she spends with Sumner, the more Bunny grows to like him, much to the chagrin of network executive Mike Cutler (Young), who starts taking Bunny a little less for granted now that there's a little competition for her affections. After a wild and drunken Christmas party, Sumner's true plans come to light—will Bunny keep her job, and can Sumner win her heart?

Critics at the time dismissed *Desk Set* as a lesser Hepburn-Tracy collaboration, but those of us who grew up watching this movie over

and over on TV feel otherwise. Their famous shared chemistry is firing on all cylinders, as they play exceedingly intelligent people who
ricochet brilliantly off each other. (Their rooftop lunch-interview is
a little marvel of zingy give-and-take.) The smart dialogue flies fast
and furious, and between the laughs you'll find yourself learning
interesting trivia tidbits about everything from the island of Corfu
to the king of the Watusis. The film's Christmas party sequence is
a blast, from Eisenhower-era alcohol abuse and sexual harassment
to the constant phone calls from tipsy co-workers demanding the
names of Santa's reindeer. (Thank goodness this film is finally available letterboxed on DVD, where Lang's split-screen telephone-call
scenes are no longer chopped up incomprehensibly by pan-and-
scan.) *Desk Set* is a delectable visit to an era when computers were
the size of large rooms and everyone didn't have instant access to the
Google.

**FUN FACTS**

- *Desk Set* screenwriters Phoebe and Henry Ephron are the parents
  of filmmaker Nora and author Delia.
- While FBC is a fictional network, its offices just happen to be located at 30 Rockefeller Plaza, home of NBC.
- EMERAC stands for Electromagnetic MEmory and Research Ar-
  ithmetical Calculator.
- The character of Bunny was based on a real-life librarian at CBS,
  Agnes Law.
- Ray Kellogg, credited with the film's "special photographic ef-
  fects," went on to direct two famously terrible low-budget mon-
  ster movies—*The Killer Shrews* and *The Giant Gila Monster* (both
  1959)—as well as John Wayne's hooray-for-the-Vietnam-War epic
  *The Green Berets* (1968).
- Tag line from the film's poster: "Meet the Desk Set . . . From 9
  O'Clock Coffee to 5 O'Clock Cocktails—And, Oh, Those Fabu-
  lous Christmas Parties!"

## *Elf* (2003)

**PG; 97 min. Written by David Berenbaum. Directed by Jon Favreau. Starring Will Ferrell, James Caan, Bob Newhart, Zooey Deschanel. (New Line Home Entertainment)**

Buddy (Ferrell) has been raised among the elves at the North Pole, but his height, gawkiness, and lack of toy-making skills make him feel like an outsider. Papa Elf (Newhart), his adoptive father, explains that Buddy crawled into Santa's sack as an infant and that he's really a human. Buddy travels to New York City to meet his father, Walter (Caan), who never knew that Buddy existed. Walter, because of his selfish and unkind management style at a children's book publishing company, is on Santa's Naughty List, but Buddy hopes to reintroduce him to the wonder of Christmas. Buddy wreaks havoc at Gimbels department store after getting into a fight with their fake Santa ("You sit on a throne of lies!") and eventually feels as out of place in Manhattan as he did in Santa's workshop, despite falling for pretty, kind-hearted Jovie (Deschanel). On Christmas Eve, though, Buddy may be the only person who can bring Walter's family together and help Santa fix his sleigh in time for his annual run.

Who would have imagined that a Christmas comedy in the jaded, cynical 21st century could be hilarious *and* sweet and sentimental *and* appropriate for all ages? Ferrell has made a career out of playing awkward naïfs, and Buddy is hands-down the most bumbling and innocent character he's ever portrayed. The romance between Buddy and Jovie is just lovely—they first bond dueting on "Baby, It's Cold Outside"—and Favreau wisely packs the cast with terrific character actors like Newhart, Caan, Ed Asner (as Santa), and Mary Steenburgen. Anyone who thinks that they don't make Christmas movies like they used to obviously hasn't seen *Elf,* a movie that manages to be both crisply modern and old-school warm and fuzzy.

**FUN FACTS**

- Favreau asked his friend and producing partner Peter Billingsley to make a cameo appearance as one of Santa's elves—and yes, that's the same Peter Billingsley who starred in *A Christmas Story* (p. 199) 20 years earlier.

- Gimbels Department Store in New York City went bankrupt in 1987; it surfaces here as an homage to *Miracle on 34th Street* (p. 207).

- The film rushed into production to take advantage of New York City's elaborate Christmas decorations, including the tree at 30 Rockefeller Plaza.

- *Elf* cost $33 million and grossed $70 million in its first ten days of release.

## *The Hebrew Hammer* (2003)

R (language, some sexual references and drug use); 85 min. Written and directed by Jonathan Kesselman. Starring Adam Goldberg, Judy Greer, Andy Dick, Mario Van Peebles. (Comedy Central Home Video)

As a child, Mordechai was the only Jewish kid at Saint Peter, Paul and Mary Elementary; he's taunted by the Gentile kids, condescended to by his bigoted teacher, and his dreidel gets stepped on by a street-corner Santa. So Mordechai grew up to be the Hebrew Hammer (Goldberg), a bad mother (shut your mouth!) who owns the streets and defends his fellow Jews. (He also dresses like a cross between a pimp and a rabbi.) When Santa Claus' evil son Damian (Dick) launches a dastardly scheme, the Jewish Justice League enlists the Hammer to save Hanukkah. Teaming up with Esther Bloomenber-gensteinenthal (Greer), and with a little help from Kwanzaa champion Mohammed Ali Paula Abdul Rahim (Van Peebles), the Hammer hopes to preserve the Festival of Lights—even if it won't impress his mother (Nora Dunn).

An outrageous spoof of 1970s blaxploitation movies and holiday films—*A Christmas Carol*'s Tiny Tim (Sean Whalen) is Damian's evil sidekick, who brainwashes Jewish children with pirated video-cassettes of *It's a Wonderful Life* (p. 202)—filtered through a hilarious Hebraic sensibility, *The Hebrew Hammer* pretty much invented the Hanukkah Movie genre. (Try getting through Adam Sandler's dreadful animated *Eight Crazy Nights* (2002) sometime, and you'll better appreciate *Hammer*'s qualities.) From its tweaking of paranoia about the "worldwide Jewish conspiracy" to the surprise revelation of the Hebrew Hammer's ultimate weapon, this movie keeps the gags coming in a constant barrage. Here's hoping the Hammer will return to save Purim or Shmini Atzeret.

**FUN FACTS**
- The script originally called for a cameo appearance by Connecticut senator Joe Lieberman, but he turned down the role; another Jewish politician makes a surprise appearance in his stead.
- Goldberg told an interviewer that he knew he had to make the film if for no other reason than to immortalize the line "Shabbat Shalom, mother****er!" onto celluloid.
- Tony Cox pops up as Jamal, one of Santa's elves—*The Hebrew Hammer* played in theaters at the same time as *Bad Santa* (p. 22), which also featured Cox in an elf costume.

## *Holiday Affair* (1949)

Unrated; 87 min. Written by Isobel Lennart, based on the story "Christmas Gift" by John D. Weaver. Directed by Don Hartman. Starring Robert Mitchum, Janet Leigh, Wendell Corey, Gordon Gebert. (Warner Home Video)

During the busy Christmas retail season, Steve (Mitchum) meets Connie (Leigh) when she buys a toy train from the department store where he works. When she comes back the next day to return it, Steve realizes that Connie is a professional shopper, sent out by a rival department store to compare prices. Because she's a war widow with a son to support and would lose her job if caught, Steve doesn't report her to management—and gets fired himself for his trouble. Steve and Connie grow close as they spend the next few days together, much to the chagrin of her stolid boyfriend Carl (Corey). Can free-spirited Steve win the love of the practical-minded Connie? And will her son Timmy (Gebert) ever be happy to see a new man in his mother's life?

As a friend pointed out, "The only way single mom Janet Leigh would turn down a successful boyfriend for an unemployed bohemian is if the bohemian is played by Robert Mitchum." So yes, for all of Steve's rootless ways and dreams of moving to California to work on boats, it helps to have the exceedingly charismatic Mitchum play the character. Freudians would have a field day with the way that Connie treats Timmy as the man of the house following her husband's death, to the point where they even call each other "Mr. Ennis" and "Mrs. Ennis." (When Connie tells Timmy that Carl has proposed, he replies, "If you marry him, you won't be Mrs. Ennis anymore!") *Holiday Affair* requires a certain suspension of disbelief, but it's worth watching for the crackling chemistry between Leigh (making one of her earliest screen appearances at age 22) and Mitchum, as well as some rather deft comic moments from Corey.

### FUN FACTS

- Poster tag line: "Mitchum's latest! It happens in December . . . but it's hotter than July!" Exhibitor guide: "Here's a romantic treat that'll take your heart for a merry sleigh ride—Mitchum playing 'santa' [*sic*] to a lovely young widow! And wait'll he finds out the mistletoe's *loaded*!"
- RKO chief Howard Hughes reportedly insisted that Mitchum play the role—a departure from his usual tough-guy characters—to

repair his public image after being arrested for marijuana posses-
sion in 1948.

## *It Happened on Fifth Avenue* (1947)

Unrated; 116 min. Written by Everett Freeman, with additional dialogue
by Vick Knight; story by Herbert Clyde Lewis and Frederick Stephani.
Directed by Roy Del Ruth. Starring Don DeFore, Gale Storm, Ann Harding, Charles Ruggles. (Warner Home Video)

Every Christmas season, millionaire Michael O'Connor (Ruggles)
boards up his Fifth Avenue mansion and winters in Virginia. And every year, while O'Connor is out of town, homeless man-about-town
Aloysius T. McKeever (Victor Moore) sneaks into his house to stave
off the winter cold. When veteran Jim (DeFore) gets evicted from his
apartment so that O'Connor's company can tear down the building
to put up a skyscraper, Aloysius invites him into the mansion. Soon,
they've got lots of company: O'Connor's daughter Trudy (Storm)
turns up to get some clothes, and the men assume that she too is
impoverished; Trudy becomes smitten with Jim, so she doesn't tell
them otherwise. Looking for Trudy, O'Connor and his estranged
wife Mary (Harding) wind up joining the household (pretending to
be poor and homeless), as do a trio of Jim's old Army pals, with their
wives and children. Will O'Connor allow his daughter to marry a
man without means? And will Jim want to marry her when she finds
out she's related to his wealthy nemesis?

When Senator Joseph McCarthy and his goons set out to look
for Communist influence in Hollywood, they no doubt went nuts
over *It Happened on Fifth Avenue*, a movie that champions the poor,
challenges the rich to rediscover their humanity and generosity,
and even celebrates the joy of communal living and the power of
collective bargaining. (Jim and his fellow veterans plan to pool
their money and purchase an abandoned army base to turn it into

apartments, not knowing that O'Connor and his board of directors have their eye on the same property.) Sadly, co-writer Lewis did eventually find himself blacklisted by the industry after McCarthy's House Un-American Activities Committee hearings, but no matter what your politics, you'll likely be charmed by the sprightly comedy and romance here, even if *It Happened on Fifth Avenue* winds up running a little long. From the sparkling performances to some hilarious bits involving an uneven restaurant table and a moth-obsessed tailor, this is a quirky and sweet holiday movie that deserves discovery.

**FUN FACTS**

- Many of the cast members went on to successful careers in television: DeFore played "Mr. B" on the long-running sitcom *Hazel*, Alan Hale Jr. (who plays one Jim's vet pals) got lost with the castaways of *Gilligan's Island*, and Storm starred on two hit programs, *My Little Margie* and *The Gale Storm Show*.
- Frank Capra's Liberty Films had originally acquired this story, but eventually abandoned it in favor of what would become *It's a Wonderful Life* (p. 202). The film received an Oscar nomination for Best Original Story but lost to another Christmas movie, *Miracle on 34th Street* (p. 207).
- The film was originally set to open at Christmas 1946 but was delayed for reasons unknown until Easter 1947.
- The song "That's What Christmas Means to Me," which debuted in *It Happened on Fifth Avenue*, became a hit for Eddie Fisher in 1952.

## *Just Friends* (2005)

PG-13; 96 min. Written by Adam Davis. Directed by Roger Kumble. Starring Ryan Reynolds, Amy Smart, Anna Faris, Chris Klein. (New Line Home Entertainment)

In 1995 New Jersey, overweight high school cheerleader Chris (Reynolds) pledges his undying love for his best friend Jamie (Smart) in her yearbook. A jock humiliates Chris by reading his words to everyone at Jamie's graduation party; she twists the knife by telling Chris, "I love you . . . like a brother." The humiliated Chris vows he'll one day become somebody important just to show them all. Ten years later, Chris is a trim and sexy record exec and a ladies' man who treats women like dirt so that they'll sleep with him and never think of him merely as a friend. En route to Paris with moronic celebutante-turned-singer Samantha (Faris), Chris' plane is forced to land in New Jersey, and he decides to spend Christmas in his hometown, with the goal of sleeping with Jamie and breaking her heart. To his surprise, Chris discovers he still loves her—can he win her from their smarmy, folk-singing classmate Dusty (Klein)? Or are Chris and Jamie doomed forever to be just friends?

Nothing is sacred in this ribald comedy, from elaborate holiday lawn displays (which get destroyed, spectacularly) to children (as a group, they tend to be pretty obnoxious in this movie, particularly when it comes to Chris' attempts to woo popular student-teacher Jamie) to the popular tearjerker *The Notebook* (which becomes the punch line of several jokes). While Reynolds is memorable as a formerly fat guy whose efforts to avenge his high school humiliations fall flat, the movie belongs to Faris, an inspired comedienne who takes the nothing role of Paris Hilton–wannabe Samantha and mines it for one brilliant comic moment after another.

### FUN FACTS

- One of the DVD's deleted sequences features Reynolds' then-girlfriend, singer Alanis Morissette, as herself.
- To get into the manic frame of mind of her character, Faris reportedly chugged Red Bulls before filming her scenes. Her metabolism probably appreciated the jump start, since temperatures on the film's Saskatchewan set dipped to 58 below.

- The story was inspired by producer Chris Bender, who spent seven years trapped in the friend zone with his future wife before they finally became romantically involved. The production couldn't get legal clearance for the name "Chris Baxter," so they went whole-hog and named the lead character "Chris Brander" in his honor.

## Love Actually (2003)

R; 135 min. Written and directed by Richard Curtis. Starring Hugh Grant, Emma Thompson, Alan Rickman, Liam Neeson. (Universal Studios Home Entertainment)

Christmastime in London sets the backdrop for a number of intertwining love stories: Karen (Thompson) worries that her marriage to Harry (Rickman) is falling apart because of his apparent flirtation with his secretary. Two of Harry's employees, Sarah (Laura Linney) and Karl (Rodrigo Santoro), try to muster up the courage to acknowledge their mutual attraction. Karen's brother David (Grant), who happens to be the new Prime Minister, finds himself falling for Natalie (Martine McCutcheon), the girl who brings in the tea. The newly widowed Daniel (Neeson) wrestles with his grief while his young stepson moons over his unrequited love for the prettiest girl in school. A goofy-looking guy travels to America in the hopes that gorgeous American babes will swoon over his British accent. A cuckolded author (Colin Firth) goes to France to work on his new book only to find himself hopelessly besotted with his maid, who speaks only Portugese, while pop singer Billy Mack (Bill Nighy) hopes for some late-in-life validation by scoring the coveted Christmas Number One slot with a cheesy, holiday-themed cover of "Love Is All Around." And so on.

If you're not a fan of the posh quippiness of Richard Curtis, then *Love Actually* isn't the movie to win you over to his charms. But if you like watching photogenic Brits juggle heartfelt emotion, zippy dialogue, and semi-excruciating social faux pas, you'll have a ball with this movie, which shockingly holds together tightly despite casting out its lines in a million directions. (There are several more subplots not even covered in the synopsis above.) There are laughs, there are tears, and there is the contemporary Western Christmas in all its tinseled glory. It's arguably indefensible on many fronts, but *Love Actually* remains shamelessly entertaining.

**FUN FACTS**

- Nighy's "Christmas Is All Around" was actually released as a single in the UK at Christmastime on the off chance that it might top the charts in real life. The Wet Wet Wet cover of the Troggs' "Love Is All Around"—featured on the soundtrack of the Curtis-scripted *Four Weddings and a Funeral* (1994)—was a huge hit in the UK with nine weeks at Number One, so Curtis was making fun of that song's ubiquity by opening *Love Actually* with another version of it.

- Believe it or not, the slender Emma Thompson is actually wearing a fat suit in the film to give her a more average-sized body.

- Two years after *Love Actually* was released, a speech delivered by real-life British prime minister Tony Blair made reference to a press conference that fake PM Grant gives in the film.

- Although this was Curtis' directorial debut, several of the cast members were already firmly entrenched in his repertory company, having appeared in projects he'd written: Grant had previously starred in *Four Weddings*, *Notting Hill* (1999), and *Bridget Jones' Diary* (2001); Thompson co-starred in the Curtis-scripted *The Tall Guy* (1989); and Rowan Atkinson (who turns in a cameo in *Love Actually* as an unctuous salesclerk) goes all the way back to Curtis' television projects, including *Mr. Bean*, *Blackadder*, and *Not the Nine O'Clock News*.

- One of the best barbs in the 2009 political comedy *In the Loop* comes when one character references the Hugh Grant character, telling a would-be political smoothie, "Shut up, *Love Actually!*"

## National Lampoon's Christmas Vacation (1989)

**PG-13; 97 min. Written by John Hughes, based on his story "Christmas '59". Directed by Jeremiah Chechik. Starring Chevy Chase, Beverly D'Angelo, Juliette Lewis, William Hickey. (Warner Home Video)**

Clark Griswold (Chase) just wants a picture-perfect family Christmas—is that too much to ask? Apparently, yes. After nearly getting killed on the freeway on his annual tree-gathering trip to the woods, he comes home with a tree so huge it takes out his living room windows and leaves Clark covered in sap. Add to that visits from two sets of squabbling in-laws, the unexpected appearance of his wife's freeloading bumpkin cousin (Randy Quaid), strings of uncooperative Christmas lights, and the threat of holiday bonuses being withheld by his cheapskate boss (Brian Doyle-Murray), and Clark becomes more manically intent on having the happiest holidays ever, even if it kills him. Or anyone else.

This third entry in the *Vacation* series was the most successful (and, for some time, the highest-grossing film with "Christmas" in the title), and while it doesn't reach the comic heights of the original movie, *Christmas Vacation* provides insight into the Clark Griswold character and why he fetishizes the idea of perfect family holidays. (Just look at his face as he watches old home movies while trapped in the attic.) The mishaps that befall the Griswold family, from the disastrous decorations to the dreadfully dry turkey to the irritating yuppie neighbors (including Julia Louis-Dreyfus, post–*Saturday Night Live* and pre-*Seinfeld*), feel very recognizable, which is probably why generations of viewers have made this manic Christmas comedy of errors a holiday favorite.

**FUN FACTS**

- The eggnog glasses that Clark and cousin Eddie drink from feature Morty Moose, the mascot of Wally World, the amusement park visited by the Griswolds in the original *Vacation* (1983).
- *Christmas Vacation* was another holiday hit for writer John Hughes, released after his Thanksgiving comedy *Planes, Trains and Automobiles* (1987) and before his Christmas smash *Home Alone* (p. 6). This film is based on his *National Lampoon* story "Christmas '59," a follow-up to "Vacation '58," the tale that inspired the original movie.
- Frank Capra III, the film's assistant director, is the grandson of the director of *It's a Wonderful Life* (p. 202) and *Meet John Doe* (p. 97).
- The Griswold home, located on the Warner Bros. lot, was also used as the Murtaugh family house in the *Lethal Weapon* (p. 253) movies.

## *Nobody's Fool* (1994)

R (some language and nudity); 110 min. Written by Robert Benton, based on the novel by Richard Russo. Directed by Robert Benton. Starring Paul Newman, Jessica Tandy, Dylan Walsh, Melanie Griffith. (Paramount Home Entertainment)

Charming old wastrel Sully (Newman) rents a room from his fourth-grade teacher Miss Beryl (Tandy), does occasional work for contractor Carl Roebuck (an unbilled Bruce Willis), steals and hides Carl's snowblower, flirts with Carl's wife Toby (Griffith), and plays a lot of poker with the colorful characters in his small town of North Bath, NY. But when Sully's long-estranged son Peter (Walsh) extends his Thanksgiving visit following a spat with his wife, Sully finds himself having to be a father to the child he'd long neglected and also a grandfather to Peter's son Wacker (Carl John Matusovich). For Sully to break his family's cycle of bad parenting, he's going to have to confront the demons of his own past. And maybe finally fix that front stoop for his landlady.

"God, I love small towns," observes one character. "Where else in the world would they let a guy out of jail for three hours just to serve as a pallbearer?" Adapting Richard Russo's novel, writer-director Benton turns the frigid hamlet of North Bath into an organic, breathing space, as full of busybodies and gossips and rivalries and love affairs and good and bad neighbors as Preston Sturges' Morgan Creek or *Gilmore Girls'* Stars Hollow. In one of the best of his latter-day screen performances, Newman proves he could still play coming-of-age characters, even in a time of life when most actors retire. Griffith and Willis reveal vulnerable, funny sides of themselves rarely captured on film, and then-newcomers Walsh, Pruitt Taylor Vince, and (as a hysterical town cop) Philip Seymour Hoffman demonstrate lots of early promise. *Nobody's Fool* is full of people you'll love getting to know, so don't be surprised to find yourself wanting to visit them every year during the holidays.

**FUN FACTS**

- Newman and Willis had worked together previously; the latter had been a bit player in *The Verdict* (1982). Willis, who was a major movie star by the time *Nobody's Fool* was released, wanted to downplay his supporting role in the film; his name appears only in the closing credits, and he worked for $1,400 a week. (He probably lost money on the film, since he bought fur-lined parkas for some members of the cast and crew because of the frigid temperatures on the upstate New York shoot.) Not that Willis didn't exercise his star prerogative: He had producers ship his personal gym from his home in L.A. to the set, and he had a clause in his contract stating he could leave immediately if his then-wife Demi Moore went into labor.

- Griffith also had a working history with Newman; she made one of her first appearances in 1976's *The Drowning Pool*. Her character's reference to "Bonnie and Clyde" in this movie has significance because Benton co-wrote the legendary 1967 film.
- Tandy died before *Nobody's Fool* reached theaters; the film is dedicated to her.

## *Nothing Like the Holidays* (2008)

**PG-13; 98 min. Written by Alison Swan and Rick Najera; story by Robert Teitel and Rene M. Rigal. Directed by Alfredo De Villa. Starring Alfred Molina, Elizabeth Peña, John Leguizamo, Vanessa Ferlito. (Anchor Bay Entertainment)**

Like all family reunions, the Rodriguez's Christmas get-together promises to be fraught with drama: Mauricio (Leguizamo) and his wife Sarah (Debra Messing) are squabbling over her putting career ahead of having babies, Jesse (Freddy Rodriguez) is home from the war in Iraq—still carrying a torch for his old girlfriend Marissa (Melonie Diaz)—and unsure if he wants to take over the family bodega, while Roxanna (Ferlito) fibs about her success as an actress in Los Angeles. But their parents Anna (Peña) and Edy (Molina) have a bombshell of their own—they're getting divorced.

This charming ensemble comedy vividly brings Chicago's Puerto Rican neighborhood of Humboldt Park to life and includes lots of great local color, including the *parranda*, an annual parade where revelers go from house to house singing Christmas carols, with the group of singers getting larger at each stop. The main strength of *Nothing Like the Holidays* lies with the extraordinary cast, which also includes Luís Guzman, Jay Hernandez, and Manny Sosa. The movie also perfectly nails the noisy dynamic of Spanish-speaking families—during a loud, squabbly dinner, Sarah asks why everyone is fighting, and Mauricio assures her that they're "just conversating." From the way the siblings rib each other and relive old rivalries to the tension between Sarah and Anna about potential grandkids, the relationships come off as smart and credible. Some of the plot twists may feel familiar, but like *This Christmas* (p. 80), this one's a must for viewers looking for a not-so-white Christmas movie.

**FUN FACTS**
- Molina is British-born but has used his fluent Spanish to good effect in films like this one and *Frida* (2002). Ferlito is Italian American.
- Despite the fact that Peña plays Leguizamo's mother, offscreen she's just three years older than he is.
- Messing and Freddy Rodriguez made their film debuts together in the 1995 melodrama *A Walk in the Clouds*.

## *Remember the Night* (1940)

Unrated; 94 min. Written by Preston Sturges. Directed by Mitchell Leisen. Starring Barbara Stanwyck, Fred MacMurray, Beulah Bondi. (Turner Classic Movies/Universal Studios Home Entertainment)

Just before Christmas, shoplifter Lee (Stanwyck) gets nabbed stealing a bracelet. New York City D.A. John (MacMurray), in a hurry to get out of town and attempting to outmaneuver Lee's attorney, demands that the trial be postponed until January so he'll have time to get an expert witness. Feeling bad that Lee will be stuck in jail over the holidays, John gets shady character Fat Mike (Tom Kennedy) to bail her out; misunderstanding John's intentions, Fat Mike hauls Lee up to John's apartment. An apologetic John takes her to dinner and discovers that they're both from Indiana, so he offers Lee a ride home to spend Christmas with her family. After a very chilly reception from Lee's mother (Georgia Caine), John takes her home with him to spend Christmas with his mother (Bondi). John and Lee grow close and discover they're fond of each other—but what's going to happen when they have to return to the courtroom on opposite sides?

It's weird to see Stanwyck and MacMurray playing such a sweet and loving couple after their immortal turn as murderous grifters in the classic *Double Indemnity* (1944), but this time around, they positively sparkle. Their road trip to Indiana has them grappling with everything from cantankerous sheriffs to overly friendly cows, and Lee blossoms with the warm reception she gets at John's house, revealing the woman she might have become under better circumstances. The snappy patter and eccentricity of the best Sturges scripts meshes perfectly with the romance and wit of Leisen (1939's *Midnight*, among many others), resulting in a holiday delight. Long unavailable on home video, the 2009 DVD release of *Remember the Night* will, with any luck, revive its status as a classic.

**FUN FACTS**

- Trees were stripped of their leaves for the farm sequence; the film is set at Christmastime, but shooting took place in July.
- MacMurray was so tall that he was forced to stand in a hole during the nightclub scene so that the camera could shoot over his shoulder when he introduces Stanwyck to the judge.
- Director Leisen made it a point to cast specific "types" in the supporting roles, since most of them have only a moment to make an impression while Stanwyck and MacMurray dominate throughout.
- This was the last screenplay written but not directed by Sturges; never completely satisfied with what other filmmakers did with his work, Sturges insisted on directing, beginning with *The Great McGinty* (1940). Not that Leisen did badly by him here; according to David Chierichetti's *Hollywood Director*, Leisen trimmed

Sturges' original 130-page screenplay to a more amenable length, excising unnecessary plot points and letting story emerge from character and dialogue. Sturges was presumably happy with Leisen's edits: Of all the films he wrote but didn't direct at Paramount, *Easy Living* (1937) and *Remember the Night* were the only ones he liked enough to purchase 16mm prints.

## Starstruck (1982)

**PG; 94 min. Written by Stephen MacLean. Directed by Gillian Armstrong. Starring Jo Kennedy, Ross O'Donovan, Margo Lee. (Blue Underground)**

Eighteen-year-old Jackie Mullins (Kennedy) dreams of being a singing star, but she's stuck working as a barmaid in a ramshackle Sydney hotel run by her mother Pearl (Lee). Angus (O'Donovan), Jackie's fast-taking 14-year-old cousin, becomes her manager, booking her to sing at an amateur night where she wows both the crowd and guitarist Robbie (Ned Lander), who falls for her. Through Angus' perseverance—which includes him convincing his cousin to do a tightrope walk between two downtown skyscrapers—Jackie gets booked on a popular teen show hosted by Terry (John O'May), whom she hopes to seduce, but it's a double fiasco: Jackie bombs singing a hackneyed ballad that Terry chooses for her, and she belatedly discovers that Terry is gay. Jackie's family celebrates Christmas at the hotel even though it looks like creditors will foreclose on them ... unless Jackie and Robbie's band can crash Terry's live New Year's Eve talent show at the Sydney Opera House and win the big $10,000 prize.

Nobody expected Armstrong's follow-up to her international smash hit *My Brilliant Career* (1979)—a literary period piece—to be a candy-colored New Wave musical, but *Starstruck*, like Armstrong's previous feature, follows a strong-willed woman who overcomes family poverty in order to pursue her artistic dreams. There's a very Mickey-and-Judy "let's put on a show" vibe to the film, and the young performers carry it off charmingly. The songs are terrific as well, from O'Donovan's "I Want to Live in a House" to Kennedy's "The Monkey in Me" to the title tune performed by the Swingers to Kennedy and O'May's "Tough." (The latter number resembles a Busby Berkeley fantasia, complete with a chorus line of Speedo-clad lifeguards swimming with rubber sharks.) North American audiences may find it unusual to see a movie where the sun is shining in December, but no matter what the weather, the Australian *Starstruck* is joyously daffy and toe-tappingly tuneful.

**FUN FACTS**
- The actor playing the floor manager at the big New Year's Eve broadcast is none other than Geoffrey Rush, a future Oscar winner for *Shine* (1996).
- Phil Judd (whose band the Swingers perform several songs in the film) and Tim Finn of Split Enz wrote the bulk of the music for *Starstruck*.
- Jackie's bit with the kangaroo suit at the amateur night is a shout-out to Marlene Dietrich stripping off a gorilla costume in *Blonde Venus* (1932).
- The stunt double who performed the actual skyscraper high-wire walk fell and had to be hospitalized.
- Kennedy went on to become a director, working in television as well as making several acclaimed short films.

## *The Sure Thing* (1985)

PG-13; 100 min. Written by Steve Bloom and Jonathan Roberts. Directed by Rob Reiner. Starring John Cusack, Daphne Zuniga, Viveca Lindfors, Anthony Edwards. (MGM Home Entertainment)

The closest thing frustrated freshman Walter "Gib" Gibson (Cusack) has had to a date during his first semester of college is a disastrous flirtation with his uptight classmate Alison Bradbury (Zuniga). So when his high school pal Lance (Edwards) calls from California to tell Gib about a "sure thing" waiting for him in L.A., Gib immediately plans to travel cross-country over Christmas break to get lucky. He finds transportation from the ride board on campus, but there are two immediate drawbacks—the drivers (Tim Robbins and Lisa Jane Persky) love to warble showtunes off-key in full volume, and his fellow passenger is Alison, who's traveling west to spend the holidays with her equally anal-retentive law student boyfriend (Boyd Gaines). The squabbling between Gib and Alison grows so intense that they get thrown out of the car and are forced to hitchhike the rest of the way to California. Through hardships, the two grow very affectionate toward one another, but when Alison discovers the reason behind Gib's trek, she's infuriated. When Gib and Alison arrive at their destination, will they separately pursue what they think they want, or will they discover that together they can find what they really need?

*The Sure Thing* travels in the deeply embedded grooves of Frank Capra's classic *It Happened One Night* (1934), but this updated spin on the material proves winning and funny enough in its own right. Director Reiner, coming off his smash debut feature *This is Spinal Tap* (1984), gets two exceedingly charismatic performances from his young romantic leads while also peppering the film with great supporting players like Persky, Robbins, and Lindfors (as Gib and Alison's free-spirited creative writing teacher). While it's ostensibly a movie about sex—Gib will climb mountains and ford streams for a night with the never-named title character played by the babelicious Nicolette Sheridan—*The Sure Thing* winds up being a love story about two opposites who fall in love not simply because the script dictates it but because, through their misadventures, they discover they're not quite so opposite after all.

**FUN FACTS**

- Reiner nods to himself by placing a *Spinal Tap* poster in Gib's dorm room; the director also dubs the voice of the cowboy singing "The Christmas Song" as well as Hercules in the cheesy movie showing on TV at the bus station. ("Stand back! Give Hercules some room!")
- While a student at Brown, co-screenwriter Roberts was one of the authors of the legendary *Official Preppy Handbook*.
- Reiner's fellow '70s sitcom veteran Henry Winkler was *The Sure Thing*'s executive producer.
- Steve Pink, who would go on to collaborate with Cusack as a writer and producer of *Grosse Pointe Blank* (1997) and *High Fidelity* (2000) and director of *Hot Tub Time Machine* (2010), makes his acting debut as "Football Player."
- Cusack had to be legally emancipated to make the film, because he hadn't yet turned 18 or graduated high school. Producer Roger Birnbaum became his legal guardian.

## *This Christmas* (2007)

**PG-13; 117 min. Written and directed by Preston A. Whitmore II. Starring Loretta Devine, Delroy Lindo, Idris Elba, Regina King. (Sony Pictures Home Entertainment)**

For propriety's sake, matriarch Shirley Ann "Ma'Dere" Whitfield (Devine) asks her longtime boyfriend Joe (Lindo) to move out of her bedroom and her house before her kids come home for Christmas, but the Whitfield children all have distractions of their own. Lisa (King), who gave up college to help run the family dry cleaning business, knows something's amiss with her husband Malcolm (Laz Alonso), but doesn't realize that he's cheating on her and cooking up a shady real estate deal on the sly with his mistress. Musician Quentin (Elba) hadn't planned to come home, but when Chicago mobsters start shaking him down to repay his debt, a trip to L.A. suddenly sounds like a great idea. Jarhead Claude (Columbus Short) has a secret or two of his own; Kelli (Sharon Leal) hopes to find a man; "professional college student" Mel (Lauren London) shows up with Devean (Keith Robinson), one in a series of new boyfriends; and Baby (Chris Brown), the youngest, wants to pursue his dream of being a singer, even though Ma'Dere—having been abandoned by the children's musician father—forbids it.

There's a whole lot of plot going on in *This Christmas*, but this breezy comedy never feels overly bogged down by the many characters and mini-dramas coursing through it. Whitmore has a feel for family dynamics, from Lisa and Kelli's squabbles (which have clearly been going on for years) to the way everyone dotes on Baby to Quentin's assumption that, as the oldest, he can still lay down the law even though no one's seen him in four years. Whitmore shares Tyler Perry's leanings toward melodrama and broad comedy—Lisa's revenge upon Malcolm is particularly memorable—but while Perry is the bigger box-office draw, Whitmore has a more assured hand as a filmmaker here; *This Christmas* has a lovely glow to it, and the performances are uniformly excellent. There's a disappointing paucity of African-American Christmas movies—unless you count *Friday After Next* (2002), an exceedingly inferior sequel in the weed-fueled comedy franchise—but here's a charmer with universal appeal.

**FUN FACTS**
- Short, Brown, and Alonso had all previously co-starred in the dance movie *Stomp the Yard* (2007)—that film and *This Christmas* were both produced by Will Packer—while Robinson, Leal, and Devine appeared together in the 2006 screen adaptation of *Dreamgirls*.
- *This Christmas* was shot in Victoria Park, a neighborhood in Los Angeles known for its stately and beautiful homes.

- Executive producer Mekhi Phifer turns in a cameo appearance as Gerald, the firefighter with eyes for Kelli.

## *29th Street* (1991)

R; 101 min. Written by George Gallo; story by Frank Pesce and James Franciscus. Directed by George Gallo. Starring Danny Aiello, Anthony LaPaglia, Lainie Kazan. (Anchor Bay Entertainment)

It's Christmas Eve, and Frank Pesce Jr. (LaPaglia) has just won $6.2 million in the very first New York State Lottery. So why is he furious, pelting snowballs at a church and lamenting his lot in life? That's what the police would like to know, so Frank tells his story: He's been lucky his entire life, ever since the night his mother gave birth to him at a hospital that wasn't the one from their neighborhood, which burned down that night. Frank Sr. (Aiello) doesn't share his son's luck, leaving him frequently in debt to the neighborhood mafiosi because of his gambling habit. After Frank Jr. becomes one of the six jackpot finalists, one of those mobsters offers to buy his lottery ticket in exchange for Frank Sr.'s debts: Will Frank Jr.'s biggest stroke of luck wind up being the one that ruins his life, or will he be able to gamble on a Christmas miracle?

Critics called *29th Street* a mix of *It's a Wonderful Life* (p. 202) and *Goodfellas* (1990), which is as good a description as any—for all its wiseguys and Little Italy color, the movie maintains a consistent sense of family ties, neighborhood togetherness, and holiday charm. You won't find much plot here, but there's a wonderfully odd (and heartwarming) sense of humor that permeates the proceedings. Frank Jr.'s luck is truly something to behold—his earnest attempts to answer the questions at his draft-board physical are so loopy that he winds up getting a psychiatric dispensation, and when he gets stabbed, the wound points doctors to a tumor in his ribs they probably would have otherwise missed. Craziest of all, this is a true story—the real Frank Jr. even co-stars in the film as his own brother.

**FUN FACTS**

- Despite the film's New York setting, much of the shooting took place in Wilmington, N.C. Many of the real-life neighborhood characters who grew up with Pesce flew down to appear in the film.
- After Gallo made a deal to make a movie telling Pesce's story, actor James Franciscus (star of TV's *Mr. Novak* and *Naked City*) came up to Gallo at a party and informed him that, because of money Franciscus had loaned to Pesce years earlier, he owned 51% of Pesce's life story. And so Franciscus received co-story and associate producer credits. Pesce had apparently also sold his life story to producers Don Simpson and Jerry Bruckheimer (*The Ref*, p. 46), who also get credits in the film.
- The project was born when Pesce played a supporting role in *Midnight Run* (1988), which Gallo wrote. He entertained cast and crew between takes telling the story of his life, and Gallo decided it was a tale worth filming.

# CHAPTER 4

Jonathan Mason and one of the three dogs playing the title role in *Lassie* (2005).

# A Blue, Blue, Blue Christmas
## HOLIDAY TEARJERKERS

Christmastime is a season of great joy, but the potent mix of nostalgia and sentimentality can just as easily bring tears to our eyes. Everyone I know who makes it a point to watch *It's a Wonderful Life* (p. 202) admits that they can't get all the way through it without bawling, so there's obviously something satisfying about the emotional release that a great tearjerker can provide over the holidays.

So it is with these films, whether they tell stories of redemption and past regrets, familial sacrifice, or longing for days gone by. Keep your holiday handkerchiefs at hand while watching these wonderful weepies.

## *All Mine to Give* (1957)

Unrated; 103 min. Written by Dale Eunson and Katherine Eunson. Directed by Allen Reisner. Starring Glynis Johns, Cameron Mitchell, Rex Thompson, Patty McCormack. (Warner Home Video)

In 1856, Scottish immigrants Mamie (Johns) and Robert (Mitchell) travel halfway around the globe to settle in Wisconsin; they've come to live with Mamie's uncle but are informed upon arrival that he has died. Soon, Mamie is pregnant, and Robert—with the help of their new neighbors—builds a cabin for their new family before winter comes. Mamie eventually gives birth to six children, and the family prospers thanks to Robert's boat-building business. Following a typhoid outbreak and the death of both Robert and Mamie, oldest son Robby (Thompson) realizes that he must find homes for his siblings—on Christmas day—before the authorities can come to take them away.

There's no shortage of movies that use Christmas as a cheap method for milking tears—*Stepmom* (1998) leaps to mind—but while *All Mine to Give* tells a devastating story, it comes by its tragedy legitimately. In other words, you'll cry, but you won't hate yourself in the morning. The film very clearly establishes the family's strong bond and work ethic, with their struggles in the barely tamed landscape tempered by their love for each other and their willingness to do what's necessary to survive. (The fact that the events in this film are based on what really happened to the ancestors of co-writer Dale Eunson perhaps provides some narrative heft to what could have been a shameless melodrama.) At just 12 years old, Robby bravely faces some of the hardest choices that anyone would have to make.

### FUN FACTS
- In 2002, Melissa Gilbert announced plans to executive-produce and star in a TV remake of the film; as of 2009, that remake remained unproduced.

- Two actresses who play sympathetic roles in the film are perhaps best known for their villainous turns elsewhere: Patty McCormack appears as Annabelle, the second-oldest child, but it's hard to look at her and not think of her indelible portrayal of homicidal moppet Rhoda Penmark in *The Bad Seed* (1956), released just one year previous. Hope Emerson, who plays friendly midwife Mrs. Pugmire, received an Oscar nomination for her turn as wicked prison matron Evelyn Harper in *Caged* (1950). (Broadway legend Glynis Johns, of course, would go on to play Kevin Spacey's obnoxious mother in *The Ref* (p. 46).)
- Tag line: "So Young . . . So Alone . . . So Courageous . . . six kids on a true, wonderful adventure! Brothers and sisters alone in the world . . . till this day each must go his own way . . . to find a home on a street where strangers live!"

## A Christmas Memory (1966)

**Unrated; 51 min. Written by Truman Capote. Directed by Frank Perry. Starring Geraldine Page, Donnie Melvin, Josip Elic. (Video Yesteryear)**

Truman Capote narrates his tale of events from his childhood that took place "more than 30 years ago." During the Depression, The Boy (Melvin) was shuttled around from relative to relative and at one point found himself living with two emotionally distant aunts. Also part of the household was a kind relation (Page) who, although advanced in years, was "still a child," according to Capote. One crisp morning, she announces that it is perfect fruitcake weather, and she and the young boy go out to gather pecans that have fallen on the ground at the pecan farm as well as the other ingredients—including whiskey, which they must purchase from bootlegger Mr. Haha (Elic)—that they have saved up all year to buy. They cut down a tree, make each other kites for Christmas, and sing carols. Soon, the boy will be sent off to military school. But he will never forget this Christmas.

In this sweet and sad nostalgia piece, Capote and director Perry—the acclaimed director of *Play It as It Lays* (1972) and *David and Lisa* (1962)—find the emotional power in the nearly plot-free narrative. Page is just perfect as the childlike woman, who makes fruitcake for President Roosevelt and is as much a victim of the cruel aunts as the little boy is. (She and the child get sweet revenge on the old biddies by noisily waking them up on Christmas morning. "Of course, they'd like to kill us both," recalls Capote, "But it's Christmas, so they can't.") This tale was remade as a feature-length TV movie in 1997—starring Eric Lloyd from *The Santa Clause* (p. 14) and Patty Duke—but it can't hold a candle to the original.

**FUN FACTS**

- *A Christmas Memory* is available on DVD in black and white, but the Paley Centers for Media in New York and Los Angeles have the original color version available for viewing.
- This film was originally produced as part of an ABC anthology series called *Stage 67*; the extraordinary crew included cinematographers Conrad Hall and Jordan Cronenweth and editor Ralph Rosenblum.
- Capote's screenplay (which featured an uncredited assist by Eleanor Perry) and Page's performance both won Emmys.

# *The Gathering* (1977)

Unrated; 94 min. Written by James Poe. Directed by Randal Kleiser. Starring Ed Asner, Maureen Stapleton, Bruce Davison, Veronica Hamel. (Warner Archive Collection)

Self-made industrial magnate Adam Thornton (Asner) learns that he has less than six months to live, so he decides to assemble his family together for one last Christmas. This is no mean feat, considering he's been estranged from his loving wife Kate (Stapleton), and she's the only one who's been keeping up with three of their four children: business-minded Tom (Lawrence Pressman), who's always been in competition with Adam; commitment-phobic career woman Peggy (Gail Strickland); and the oldest, Bud (Gregory Harrison), who's been living in Canada ever since he dodged the draft despite Adam's disapproval. Only daughter Julie (Rebecca Balding) stayed close to Adam after he and Kate split up. Adam laments that Christmas has gone to "phony plastic trees, electronic music, smog, and black slush," but—keeping his condition a secret from everyone in the family besides Kate—he'll do everything he can for one last New England Christmas with his family.

*The Gathering* uses Adam's imminent demise to get its story in motion but never exploits it—he doesn't die over the course of the story, and since few other characters know of his terminal condition, there's a minimum of boo-hooing. Christmas movies are often at their best when they tell stories of personal redemption, and that's certainly what happens here; having a literal deadline finally motivates Adam to get his house in order and to repair the many broken relationships in his life. One of the film's strong points is that there aren't really any villains in it: Adam's children have legitimate reasons for disliking their father, and it's up to him to win back their love.

**FUN FACTS**

- One of Bud's concerns about coming back home for Christmas is the possibility of arrest; draft dodgers were subject to prosecution until January 1977, when President Jimmy Carter (on his first day in office) signed an executive order pardoning everyone who went to Canada to avoid being drafted into the Vietnam War.
- Joseph Barbera, who executive-produced *The Gathering*—and its inferior sequel, *The Gathering, Part II* (1979)—is best known as half of the animation team Hanna-Barbera, who gave us *Scooby-Doo*, *The Flintstones*, and *Yogi Bear*, among countless others.

- Adam reads a ribald poem called "Christmas Day in the Work-house," and while he attributes it to Kipling, it's actually a drinking song from World War II that parodies George R. Sims' "In the Workhouse Christmas Day."
- *The Gathering* fell between two high-profile collaborations of director Kleiser and John Travolta—the Emmy-winning TV movie *The Boy in the Plastic Bubble* (1976) and the smash hit musical *Grease* (1978).

## *Heidi* (1937)

**G; 88 min. Written by Walter Ferris and Julien Josephson, based on the novel by Johanna Spyri. Directed by Allan Dwan. Starring Shirley Temple, Jean Hersholt, Mary Nash, Marcia Mae Jones. (20th Century Fox Home Entertainment)**

After the death of her parents, young Heidi (Temple) is taken by her cruel Aunt Dete (Mady Christians) to live with Heidi's grandfather (Hersholt), a hermit who lives in a tiny house in the Alps. "The Grandfather," as Heidi calls him, had forbidden Heidi's parents to marry and thus is not happy to have her in his home. But Heidi's joy and adoration work their way through his rough exterior, and he soon becomes kind not only to the girl but also to the local villagers who had once feared him. Soon after Grandfather's transformation, Dete returns and kidnaps Heidi, taking her to Frankfurt to be a companion to Klara (Jones), a young invalid. While Grandfather searches for her, Heidi's charms win over Klara and her wealthy father. But cruel housekeeper Fraulein Rottenmeier (Nash) has nefarious plans for Heidi. Can Grandfather find her before Christmas?

   If you've never sat down and experienced the dynamo that was young Shirley Temple, start with *Heidi*; through some miracle, Temple portrays a sunny and upbeat character without ever

overdoing it and turning the movie into a sap-fest. (Her performance is almost the juvenile, subtext-free equivalent of Sally
Hawkins' Oscar-nominated turn in 2008's *Happy-Go-Lucky*.)
Temple wins over audience members the same way Heidi melts
the hearts of the grumpy people around her. The film's climax is
almost unbearably suspenseful, with Grandfather trying to find
little Heidi in the big city while the thoroughly wicked Fraulein
Rottenmeier is trying to sell the girl to gypsies. With its mix of
humor, pathos, music, and suspense, *Heidi* will enrapture viewers
of all ages.

**FUN FACTS**

- The film's Alpine settings were shot entirely at Lake Arrowhead,
  Calif., during the summer. Hersholt's heavy woolen costumes
  caused him to collapse from heat exhaustion. Temple herself
  missed a few days of shooting after becoming ill from accidentally
  swallowing fake snow during one of the winter scenes.
- The "In Our Little Wooden Shoes" musical sequence was actually
  added to the film at Temple's behest. She was just nine years old
  upon *Heidi*'s release, but the film's success made her Hollywood's
  top-drawing box-office star for the third year in a row. She was
  later named U.S. ambassador to Ghana (1974) and the former
  Czechoslovakia (1989).
- That's a real look of surprise on Temple's face when the goat
  squirts milk in her face; without telling her, director Dwan attached a tube to the goat's udder that Temple couldn't see, then
  squirted her in the face once the cameras were rolling.

## *The Homecoming: A Christmas Story* (1971)

**PG; 100 min. Written by Earl Hamner Jr., based on his novel. Directed
by Fielder Cook. Starring Richard Thomas, Patricia Neal, Cleavon Little, Ellen Corby. (Paramount Home Video)**

It is Christmas Eve, 1933, and the Walton family wonders whether their father (Andrew Duggan) will make it home in time for the holidays. (Ever since the local mill closed down, he has to travel miles away for work, returning home only on the weekends.) Oldest son John-Boy (Thomas) does his best to keep his younger brothers and sisters from worrying too much about their father's absence, while his mother (Neal), having heard news on the radio of a fatal bus accident on a route her husband often travels, tries to distract herself by preparing her famous applesauce cake. Meanwhile, a "Robin Hood" bandit steals groceries and gives them to poor people, a condescending religious missionary from the big city brings shabby toys for the impoverished children, and two elderly maidens (who also happen to be the local moonshiners) try to help John-Boy find his father before Christmas comes.

The movie that launched the beloved TV series *The Waltons* (which ran on CBS from 1972-1981, not counting various reunion movies), *The Homecoming*—much like *A Christmas Memory* (p. 87) before it—beautifully captures Christmas during the Depression and how resourceful people did what they could to make spirits bright despite limited means. (Bob Cratchit would be proud.) Neal's a legendary actress—though she lacks the warmth of Michael Learned, who would go on to play Ma Walton in the series, her scenes with Thomas have real heft. (Good luck keeping your eyes dry, incidentally, when John-Boy opens his Christmas present.) Brimming over with colorful characters, sibling squabbles, and poignant drama, *The Homecoming* is a Christmas must-see even for those who never watched the series that followed.

**FUN FACTS**

- The Waltons gather around the radio to listen to *Fibber McGee & Molly*, but that show didn't premiere until 1935.
- Hamner's novel *Spencer's Mountain* had previously been turned into a 1963 film of the same name, starring Henry Fonda. Hamner's

childhood in Schuyler, Va., provided inspiration for the novel and for many of the other stories told over the course of *The Waltons'* ten-year run.

- The oft-parodied "Good night, John-Boy" ending of every episode of *The Waltons* makes its first appearance at the climax of *The Homecoming.*

## I'll Be Seeing You (1944)

**Unrated; 85 min. Written by Marion Parsonnet, based on the play by Charles Martin. Directed by William Dieterle. Starring Ginger Rogers, Joseph Cotten, Shirley Temple, Spring Byington. (MGM Home Video)**

Mary (Rogers) and Zachary (Cotten) meet on a train at Christmastime, and each of them seems to be keeping a secret—she doesn't know that the war has made chocolate hard to come by, and he has a hard time buying a magazine. It turns out that Mary has been in jail for several years and is visiting relatives over the holidays on a good-behavior furlough. Zachary, a decorated war hero, has been suffering post-traumatic stress disorder from his experiences in combat; he's using a ten-day leave from the hospital to expose himself to the outside world to see whether or not he's capable of living outside of a mental institution. Can these two damaged individuals find love despite their current predicaments?

For all its trappings of a soapy "woman's picture," *I'll Be Seeing You* takes the kind of tough look at real-life situations that were more likely to be explored in noir films. Mary's in prison for manslaughter, despite the fact that she committed the crime in self-defense against her boss, who was about to physically assault her; Zachary is constantly reminded of—and traumatized by—his wartime experiences, and the subject of "battle fatigue" was one that wasn't being discussed that much at the time. (There's also a terrific, and timely, scene where a senator glad-hands war hero Zachary for his opinion on political issues; refusing to speak for the whole army, Zachary responds, "I haven't the slightest idea what a lot of soldiers think.") Rogers and Cotten are just right as the vulnerable leads, and Temple gives a moving adolescent performance as Mary's judgmental cousin who comes to appreciate and understand everything that Mary has been through.

See also: *Since You Went Away* (1944), another film from the same year that also starred Cotten and Temple. A look at how the war was affecting the wives and children left behind by soldiers—Claudette Colbert, Jennifer Jones, and Temple play a family struggling with the financial and emotional repercussions that occur when the man of the house goes overseas—this tearjerker features a memorable climax at Christmastime.

**FUN FACTS**

- Mary at first tells Zachary that she works as a traveling saleslady; Rogers later starred in the comedy *The First Traveling Saleslady* (1956).
- George Cukor was originally slated to direct and was later replaced by Dieterle. Joan Fontaine planned to play the lead but had to withdraw because of previous commitments.
- John Derek plays the young officer who escorts Shirley Temple's character to the New Year's dance; he would later direct his wife Bo Derek in such infamous softcore duds as *Tarzan the Ape Man* (1981) and *Bolero* (1984).

## *Joyeux Noël (Merry Christmas)* (2005)

PG-13; 116 min. Written and directed by Christian Carion. Starring Diane Kruger, Benno Fürmann, Daniel Brühl. (Sony Pictures Home Entertainment)

On Christmas Eve 1914, three armies gather along World War I's Western front in France as Scottish and French forces unite to assault the German trenches. German tenor Nikolaus Sprink (Fürmann), now a soldier, reunites with his wife Anna (Kruger) when the two of them perform a Christmas concert for generals at headquarters. Sprink insists on returning to the front lines to sing for the men, and Anna accompanies him. When they arrive, the Scots are singing "I'm Dreaming of Home," accompanied by bagpipers. When the Sprinks sing "Adeste Fideles," the pipers play for them, and the Germans bring their lit Christmas trees out from the trenches and onto the battlefield. And so begins a temporary truce, in which soldiers will find common ground, the dead will be recovered and buried, and officers of three armies will get a glimpse of brotherhood amidst the lunacy of war.

The film begins with schoolboys of various European nations reciting poems that praise their homeland and vilify their enemies, and we see how these deep-seeded hostilities reached full flower in "the war to end all wars." But the Christmas truce—an actual historical event that took place a few months into World War I, although all countries involved did their best to bury the facts for decades—demonstrated that, even if nations have a hard time finding common ground, the men who fight the wars certainly can. In an era where an Anglican bishop could, from the pulpit, accuse Germans of crucifying babies, and in a war when a cat was actually arrested and shot for treason for "consorting with the enemy," the fact that peace could be achieved for even a few days has to rate as an actual Christmas miracle.

## FUN FACTS

- Director Carion had to shoot the film in Romania because no French military base wanted to be associated with the "rebellion" that took place in 1914.
- This same historical incident inspired the video for Paul McCartney's "Pipes of Peace," in which the singer plays both a British and a German officer.

- France's selection of *Joyeux Noël* as its Oscar entry that year caused a minor scandal, since the film hadn't yet opened in its home country (apart from a one-week release in northern France), violating the rule that the nominee had to have recorded 200,000 admissions to qualify.

## *Lassie* (2005)

**PG; 100 min. Written by Charles Sturridge, based on the novel *Lassie Come Home* by Eric Knight. Directed by Charles Sturridge. Starring Jonathan Mason, Peter O'Toole, Samantha Morton. (Genius Products)**

In England on the eve of World War II, an impoverished Yorkshire family must sell young Joe's (Mason) beloved dog Lassie to the Duke (O'Toole). Lassie, as smart as she is beautiful, escapes the Duke's estate over and over again to return to her beloved Joe, who must eventually lie to the dog and tell her he no longer loves her so that she will stop escaping. The Duke then takes her up to Scotland, but Lassie eludes the Duke's cruel kennel-man and begins the long trek back to Yorkshire, and to Joe. Along the way, she encounters everything from the Loch Ness monster to a traveling entertainer (Peter Dinklage). Will Lassie make it home in time for Christmas?

Kids and adults alike will have a good Christmas cry with this moving and ultimately joyous boy-and-his-dog tale. The thought of another Lassie adventure may have you cringing, but this is the kind of literate, intelligent kids' movie—like *The Black Stallion* (1979) and *The Secret Garden* (1993)—that comes along all too rarely. Charles Sturridge wrote a powerful adaptation of the original *Lassie* novel and then populated his cast with a mix of veteran U.K. actors (O'Toole, Morton, John Lynch, Kelly Macdonald) and talented newcomers (Mason, as well as Hester Odgers in the role of the Duke's granddaughter). The result is a stirring adventure that's bound to become a holiday favorite in dog-loving households everywhere.

**FUN FACTS**

- This adaptation returned Lassie to her roots—the 1940 novel *Lassie Come Home*, which began as a series of stories in the *Saturday Evening Post* in 1938. When Sturridge was hired to write the film, he had no idea there ever was a book or that it was originally a British story, his knowledge of *Lassie* having been limited to the American TV series of the 1950s.
- Three dogs were used during filming—what the animal coordinator called "the stunt dog, the running dog, and the picture dog"—and vegetable dyes were used to make the three look identical. The "picture dog" was a descendant of "Pal," the legendary canine performer who originally played Lassie in 1943's *Lassie Come Home*, opposite Elizabeth Taylor.

## *Meet John Doe* (1941)

**Unrated; 122 min. Written by Robert Riskin; story by Richard Connell and Robert Presnell. Directed by Frank Capra. Starring Gary Cooper, Barbara Stanwyck, Walter Brennan, Edward Arnold. (Sony Pictures Home Entertainment and other sources)**

Newspaper columnist Ann Mitchell (Stanwyck) gets fired by her paper's new owners; they want "fireworks" and her stuff is too "lavender and old lace." So she writes her last column about John Doe, an out-of-work guy who plans to jump off the roof of City Hall on Christmas Eve to protest the unemployment situation. John Doe is completely made up—shades of Stanwyck's prevaricating journalist in *Christmas in Connecticut* (p. 57)—but the column is such a sensation that the public pressures her to produce him. Ann and her editors audition several homeless drifters and wind up selecting former baseball player Long John Willoughby (Cooper), who's happy to be earning some money and getting regular meals. John's traveling companion The Colonel (Walter Brennan) thinks they should get out while the getting is good, but John falls for Ann and decides to stick around. The John Doe movement becomes a nationwide phenomenon, but when John resists being used by a powerful politician (Arnold), everything comes crashing down. Will John jump off of City Hall on Christmas Eve to keep the message of John Doe alive?

One of director Frank Capra's populist masterpieces, *Meet John Doe* wonderfully depicts the concerns of the average American—all the John Does out there—in contrast to the greed and corruption of corporate interests and the politicians they control. Cooper and Stanwyck make a great screen pairing, and—as in most of Capra's best films—there's exceptional casting, all the way down to the tiniest roles. Every soda jerk and small-town housewife in the movie makes a decided impact, no matter how briefly they appear on screen. One of John's best lines reminds us of the appeal of so many of the films we go back and watch every December: "There's something swell about the spirit of Christmas, to see what it does to people, all kinds of people. Now why can't that spirit, that same warm Christmas spirit, last the whole year 'round?"

## FUN FACTS

- The climactic City Hall scene was filmed in a rented icehouse at temperatures of 12 degrees, so that the actors' breath would be visible when they spoke.
- Capra didn't want anyone but Cooper for the lead role; the two had previously collaborated on the hit *Mr. Deeds Goes to Town* (1936). *Meet John Doe* was Capra's last film before World War II; the director joined the Army and made a series of wartime propaganda films known collectively as *Why We Fight*.
- A musical version of *Meet John Doe* was staged at Ford's Theatre in Washington, D.C., in 2007.
- *Meet John Doe* was one of 13 films directed by Capra that featured story and/or screenplay by Riskin.

# 3 Godfathers (1948)

**Unrated; 106 min. Written by Laurence Stallings and Frank S. Nugent; story by Peter B. Kyne. Directed by John Ford. Starring John Wayne, Pedro Armendáriz, Harry Carey Jr., Ward Bond. (Warner Home Video)**

Three men—Robert (Wayne), Pedro (Armendáriz), and the Abilene Kid (Carey)—arrive in Welcome, AZ just before Christmas. They chat with Buck Sweet (Bond); the newcomers don't know he's the sheriff, and he doesn't know they're in town to rob the bank. As the desperadoes flee from town, Marshall Sweet shoots one of their water bags, leaving them to go into the desert with just one canteen. Trying to guess their next move based on their need for water, Marshall Sweet has no way of knowing that the criminals' plans will have to change when they encounter a tenderfoot's widow (Mildred Natwick) who's about to give birth. (Unbeknownst to them, she is Marshall Sweet's niece.) She barely survives the experience, but lives long enough to name the baby after the three men. Can these Magi of the old west transport the child to safety and civilization before they die of thirst?

The Abilene Kid makes a specific reference to the Three Wise Men of the first Christmas, but it's a connection that everyone else in the audience has already made. Still, this John Ford adventure turns the Christmas story on its ear, replacing the Virgin Mary with a woman who won't live to reach her intended destination on the prairie and substituting three outlaws for Caspar, Balthazar, and Melchior. Lots of Westerns have chases and bank holdups and desperate men making their way through the desert, but how many of them show cowboys washing a newborn with olive oil or changing diapers? It's a tale of love and sacrifice amid the shootouts.

See also: The original story was previously filmed by director William Wyler as *Hell's Heroes* (1930); the animated feature *Tokyo Godfathers* (2003) puts an interesting spin on the material, transposing it to modern-day Japan, with three homeless people (one of whom is a cross-dresser) finding and rescuing an abandoned infant.

**FUN FACTS**

- Harry Carey Jr.'s father was a close friend of Ford's and starred in *The Three Godfathers* (1916), a silent version of this story; *3 Godfathers* is dedicated to the elder Carey's memory. (Ford himself had previously filmed the tale as 1919's *Marked Men*; that film is thought to be lost.)
- Wayne was so badly sunburned during production that he had to be briefly hospitalized.
- Ford cast many of his regular players in the film, from Wayne and Bond to Jane Darwell, Ben Johnson, and Mae Marsh. (Marsh, who plays Mrs. Sweet, was by that point one of the cinema's most established stars—she was second-billed to Lillian Gish in D. W. Griffith's *Birth of a Nation* [1915].)

# CHAPTER 5

Billy Bob Thornton and John Cusack in *The Ice Harvest* (2005).

# Putting the Heist Back in Christmas
## CRIME & ACTION EXTRAVAGANZAS

The charitable fund-raisers in *A Christmas Carol* (see Chapter 7) refer to the holiday as a time "when Want is keenly felt, and Abundance rejoices," and it's the larceny-tempting chasm between Want and Abundance that fuels these films, action-filled crime dramas that take place against a backdrop of generosity and plenty. Too bad Bob Cratchit never masterminded a daring mission to break into the safe at Scrooge and Marley while the office was closed on December 25.

Christmas serves as a backdrop for these films in varied ways. Sometimes, directors just want to cover their sets in shiny toys, twinkling lights, and plastic snowmen; other films present dastardly deeds in sharp contrast to the season of love and sharing and understanding, delighting in the friction between absolute goodness and awesome gunplay. All of them are a reminder that the definition of "Christmas movie" isn't limited to sentimental stories about kids and puppies and Santa Claus.

## *Batman Returns* (1992)

PG-13; 126 min. Written by Daniel Waters; story by Waters and Sam Hamm, based on characters created by Bob Kane. Directed by Tim Burton. Starring Michael Keaton, Michelle Pfeiffer, Danny DeVito, Christopher Walken. (Warner Home Video)

It's Christmastime in Gotham City, and all manner of creatures are running wild. First there's the grotesque Penguin (DeVito), abandoned by his wealthy parents in infancy and raised by penguins in the sewer. While he pursues his own twisted vengeance upon polite society, department store magnate Max Shreck (Walken) plans to build a power plant that will rob the city's energy. (This guy was Enron before we knew what Enron was really about.) And if Shreck has to make the Penguin mayor of Gotham to get his way, he's prepared to do so. Also in the mix is Catwoman (Pfeiffer), who, as mousy secretary Selina Kyle, figured out Shreck's nefarious scheme and got pushed out a high window by him for her troubles. Now she's got feline powers—and a killer catsuit—and she's out for revenge. Can Batman (Keaton) stop this trio of no-goodniks?

After the smash success of Tim Burton's *Batman* (1989), a sequel was inevitable, but no one expected that the director would take his dark and brooding vision of the venerable comic book character even further into the shadows. Audiences expecting a family-friendly film were shocked—the fact that McDonald's had Happy Meal tie-ins became a major subject of media disapproval—but fans loved the creepier storyline and the fact that Burton decorated his Expressionist Gotham with snow and festive décor. Pfeiffer's Catwoman made a much more interesting romantic counterpart for Batman than Kim Basinger's Vicki Vale in the first movie, and in general *Batman Returns* ranks among the rare sequels that are actually superior to their predecessor. This forbidding and shadowy world is an odd place for holiday cheer, but the sharp juxtaposition makes the Christmas element that much more fun to look at—it's this unlikely mix, in fact, that makes *Batman Returns* something of a dress rehearsal for the Burton-produced *The Nightmare Before Christmas* (p. 209).

## FUN FACTS

- The Max Shreck character is a reference to actor Max Schreck, who portrayed the titular vampire in F. W. Murnau's Expressionist masterpiece *Nosferatu* (1922).
- All the bats that appear in the film are computer-generated, but the penguins are a mix of real African Penguins and King Penguins with some robots, CG birds, and even men in penguin suits thrown in as well.
- The Cobblepots—the Penguin's parents, who abandon him Moses-style at the beginning of the film—are played by Paul Reubens and Diane Salinger, who appeared in Burton's first feature, *Pee-wee's Big Adventure* (1985).
- Actress Sean Young—who was to have played Vicki Vale in Burton's *Batman* before a collarbone injury forced her to drop out—infamously showed up at the director's office in a homemade Catwoman suit, insisting on being tested for the role; he managed to elude her.
- Co-writer Daniel Waters got the idea of having Penguin run for mayor from one of the episodes of the campy 1960s *Batman* TV show.

# Die Hard (1988)

R; 131 min. Written by Jeb Stuart and Steven E. de Souza, based on the novel *Nothing Lasts Forever* by Roderick Thorp. Directed by John McTiernan. Starring Bruce Willis, Bonnie Bedelia, Alan Rickman, Hart Bochner. (20th Century Fox Home Entertainment)

New York cop John McClane (Willis) travels to Los Angeles to spend Christmas with estranged wife Holly (Bedelia) and their children.

Upon McClane's arrival at LAX, driver Argyle (De'voreaux White) takes him directly to Nakatomi Plaza, where Holly's company is throwing its big holiday office party. Amidst the festivities, terrorist Hans Gruber (Rickman) and his accomplices show up to hold the Nakatomi employees hostage and to demand the release of political prisoners around the world. Alas, terrorism is just a front for what turns out to be an exceedingly clever plan to rob the company vaults at Nakatomi, but the one thing Gruber didn't prepare for was the presence of McClane, who keeps to the shadows and does what he can to foil the evildoers. With the LAPD and the FBI gathering outside and Gruber growing more desperate, can McClane stop the bad guys and save his wife?

In its own way, *Die Hard* is as perfect a movie as *Casablanca*, blessed with a standout cast (including such stellar character actors as Reginald VelJohnson, William Atherton, Paul Gleason, James Shigeta, and Robert Davi) and one of the smartest action-movie scripts ever written. Stuart and de Souza pepper the film with great lines—after Gruber demands the release of members of an obscure group called Asian Dawn, he admits to a comrade that he "heard about them on *60 Minutes*"—and the kind of payoffs you'd expect in a perfectly timed French farce. For instance, the person sitting next to McClane on the plane tells him the best way to adjust after flying is to take off your socks and shoes and make fists with your toes; this action sets up McClane to be barefoot for the rest of the movie, which becomes an issue once the windows at Nakatomi start shattering. In another example, John is saddened when he learns Holly has been using her maiden name at the office; this becomes important later as it keeps Gruber from immediately discovering the link between hostage Holly and fly-in-the-ointment John. Best of all, Gruber's robbery plans are not only brilliantly crafted, but they're also perfectly logical, unlike so many villainous movie schemes. *Die Hard* was the first film that gave Willis a character that perfectly fit his on-screen persona, but it's Rickman's dangerously cosmopolitan villain who steals the show. And even the Christmas setting isn't a throwaway—in the classic tradition of Christmas-movie leading men, John McClane undergoes a sort of redemption, learning to appreciate his wife and to see her in a new light. Oh, and the climactic shootout involves gift wrap.

See also: What's the most terrifying place to be on Christmas Eve? An airport, of course, which is just part of what makes *Die Hard 2* (1990) almost as suspenseful as its predecessor. This time, McClane's got his hands full with some renegade U.S. soldiers out to liberate a South American drug lord being transferred Stateside to face trial, while Holly (and Atherton's self-serving TV journalist) are circling the airport in a plane that's dangerously close to running out of fuel.

**FUN FACTS**
- Thorp's novel *Nothing Lasts Forever* was the sequel to his book *The Detective*, which was made into a 1968 movie starring Frank Sinatra; if it's exceedingly difficult to imagine Sinatra's and Willis' characters being the same guy, it's because neither interpretation hews too closely to the cop from the novels.
- By the late '80s, Atherton (who plays a smarmy TV journalist) and Gleason (as a useless police officer) were already famous as two of the screen's greatest smug jerks; Atherton was the foil to the *Ghostbusters* in 1984 while Gleason played the obnoxious principal who tormented *The Breakfast Club* (1985).
- The scene where Gruber fools McClane into thinking that he's one of the hostages was added during production after McTiernan realized that Rickman could do a killer American accent. And the surprised look on Rickman's face when he takes a fall toward the end of the film is genuine; McTiernan had the actor dropped a second early, which infuriated Rickman.
- "Nakatomi Plaza" can be seen on your next visit to Los Angeles; it's actually the Fox Plaza building in Century City.

- Some theaters pulled the *Die Hard* trailer in the spring of 1988 because audiences—who weren't big fans of Willis' two previous movies, *Sunset* (1988) and *Blind Date* (1987)—booed whenever he appeared on screen. Willis got the last laugh, though, with *Die Hard* becoming a huge hit during the same summer that new action movies from Sylvester Stallone (*Rambo III*), Arnold Schwarzenegger (*Red Heat*), Clint Eastwood (*The Dead Pool*), and Sean Connery (*The Presidio*) all underperformed.

- The popularity of *Die Hard* not only led to three sequels (to date) but to an entire sub-genre of action movies about people trapped somewhere having to overcome bad guys, with *Speed* (1994) referred to as "*Die Hard* on a bus" and *Under Siege* (1992) as "*Die Hard* on a battleship," et. al. Hollywood legend has it that someone eventually tried to pitch "*Die Hard* in a building" to a major studio.

- Film critic Pauline Kael noted that *Die Hard* has holiday appeal beyond its setting: "In a strange way, this picture's mixture of sentimentality and violence defines Hollywood's version of the Christmas spirit: you get a lot of expensive toys and smash them all to pieces, because you know there are a lot more where they came from."

## D.O.A. (1988)

**R; 96 min. Written by Charles Edward Pogue; based on a screenplay by Russell Rouse and Clarence Greene. Directed by Rocky Morton and Annabel Jankel. Starring Dennis Quaid, Meg Ryan, Daniel Stern, Charlotte Rampling. (Walt Disney Home Video)**

Professor Dexter Cornell (Quaid) goes to the police to report a murder—his own. Someone has poisoned Dexter, and he's got just 24 hours to figure out whodunit. That's not the only mystery in Dexter's life, however, since one of his most promising students, Nick Lang

(Robert Knepper), just jumped off the roof of a building after asking Dexter to read his first novel. Was Nick having an affair with Dexter's soon-to-be-ex-wife Gail (Jane Kaczmarek)? Was Nick also involved with Cookie Fitzwaring (Robin Johnson), even though Cookie's mother (Rampling) had adopted Nick and was putting him through college? And why has Dexter's young student Sydney (Ryan) waited until the end of the semester to get flirty with her prof?

A remake of the gritty 1950 B-movie of the same name (which isn't a Christmas movie), *D.O.A.* embraces the shadowy world of film noir, despite being shot in color and set in sunny Austin, Tex. Even with the holidays just around the corner, everyone's sweating up a storm, adding to the tension and claustrophobia of this ultimate ticking-clock thriller. The eggnog and tinsel are among the many incongruous ingredients of this crafty mystery, visually styled to a fare-thee-well by directors Rocky Morton and Annabel Jankel, previously known for their music videos and the 1980s *Max Headroom* TV series. Quaid, as a washed-up novelist who hides his writer's block behind a façade of cynicism and bitterness, makes a perfect noir narrator, and his chemistry with Ryan—whom he would marry three years later—feels as tangible as the Texas humidity. And Rampling, naturally, was born to play the role of a femme fatale with a dark secret in her past. *D.O.A.* wasn't a big hit, but it's a stylish and entertaining nail-biter. (It also features one of the corniest Christmas-related riddles ever told, but you'll have to hear it for yourself.)

**FUN FACTS**
- That's one-hit wonder Timbuk 3 ("The Future's So Bright, I Gotta Wear Shades") as the bar band playing at Austin's famous Continental Club when Dexter and Cookie share martinis.
- *D.O.A.* wasn't screenwriter Pogue's only remake—he's probably most famous for co-writing David Cronenberg's 1986 take on *The Fly*. (That same year, Pogue also wrote the horror sequel *Psycho III*.)

# *Go* (1999)

**R; 102 min. Written by John August. Directed by Doug Liman. Starring Sarah Polley, Katie Holmes, Scott Wolf, Jay Mohr. (Sony Pictures Home Entertainment)**

We see the events of a riotous Christmas Eve in Los Angeles and Las Vegas from various perspectives. Grocery cashier Ronna (Polley) tries selling ecstasy to TV actors Zack (Mohr) and Adam (Wolf) but, sensing a police trap, she flushes the pills down the toilet; to pay back dealer Todd (Timothy Olyphant), she goes to a rave and sells diet pills and chewable aspirin to gullible clients. Zack and Adam participate in the aborted ecstasy deal to get the police off their backs, only to find out that cop Burke (William Fichtner) has another agenda in mind. Ronna's fellow employee Simon (Desmond Askew) gets into trouble in Las Vegas that involves a stolen car and gun, a burning hotel room, some angry strip club employees, and Todd's credit card. As we jump forwards and backwards in time, these disparate stories come together in surprising and hilarious ways.

There's no easy way to synopsize the sprawling and coincidence-heavy plot of *Go*, and maybe that's why this smart, stylish, and funny action-comedy wasn't a bigger hit upon its original release. But even though raves are now nearly as dated as love-ins, this movie gets better and better with each passing year. For one thing, director Doug Liman—who would go on to make *The Bourne Identity* (2002) and *Mr. & Mrs. Smith* (2005)—assembled a cast of talented young actors who were just starting to get established in the business, most of whom had bright futures awaiting them. And then there's John August's crafty script, which manages not only to get plate after plate aloft but also to keep them all spinning, all the while creating dissonance between its holiday setting and its characters who, quite simply, brazenly ignore it. (You'll forget enough of the twists between viewings to make *Go* worth watching multiple times.)

**FUN FACTS**
- Liman first gained fame as a filmmaker as the director of the cult hit comedy *Swingers* (1996), which also shuttles back and forth between Los Angeles and Las Vegas.
- Christina Ricci, originally cast in the film, dropped out and was replaced by Sarah Polley.
- The *Go* script, screenwriter August's first produced screenplay, was inspired by the clerks at a Sunset Blvd. grocery store known locally as "rock and roll Ralph's."

## *The Ice Harvest* (2005)

R; 92 min. Written by Richard Russo and Robert Benton, based on the novel by Scott Phillips. Directed by Harold Ramis. Starring John Cusack, Billy Bob Thornton, Connie Nielsen, Oliver Platt. (Universal Pictures Home Entertainment)

Charlie Arglist (Cusack) and Vic Cavanaugh (Thornton) have stolen two million dollars from Charlie's client, mob boss Bill Guerrard (Randy Quaid) on Christmas Eve. All they have to do is sit tight and stay quiet before they leave town at dawn, but the night that follows is anything but silent. Charlie flirts with stripper Renata (Nielsen), gets involved in a plot to blackmail a local city councilman, shuttles around his friend Pete (Platt)—who has married Charlie's shrike of an ex-wife—and does his best to avoid Roy (Mike Starr), an enforcer who wants Guerrard's money back. Over the course of the evening, Charlie discovers there's no one he can trust and learns that people will do just about anything to each other when there's two million dollars at stake.

Forget "White Christmas"—the bleak, frozen Wichita, Kans., setting of *The Ice Harvest* is constantly grey, slushy, and rainy, the official weather of Seasonal Affective Disorder. This exceedingly dark comedy may feature the star of *The Sure Thing* (p. 78) and a script from the writers of *Nobody's Fool* (p. 72), but it's nothing like either of those films, instead serving up characters who embody the worst in people; all seven of the deadly sins are repeatedly committed over the course of one December 24, but the cast is so committed to the material that they make this gruesomely sardonic bit of business— much like *Bad Santa* (p. 22), also starring Thornton—the perfect holiday alternative for viewers who've heard one "God bless us, every one" too many. (The DVD features several alternate endings that would have made the movie even darker.)

**FUN FACTS**
- Focus Features' marketing department sent copies of the DVD encased in a block of ice to members of the press.
- Nielsen took over the role of Renata after actress Monica Bellucci dropped out due to pregnancy.

## *Kiss Kiss Bang Bang* (2005)

R; 102 min. Written by Shane Black, based on the novel *Bodies Are Where You Find Them* by Brett Halliday. Directed by Shane Black. Starring Robert Downey Jr., Val Kilmer, Michelle Monaghan, Larry Miller. (Warner Home Video)

On the run from the NYPD, petty thief Harry (Downey) ducks into what turns out to be an open casting call for a movie—and he's so hyped-up and intense from the chase that he lands the part. Next thing Harry knows, he's in Los Angeles and prepping for his role as a detective by tailing real-life private dick Gay Perry (Kilmer). Harry crosses paths with aspiring actress Harmony (Monaghan), and after the two exchange some hilarious pick-up banter in a bar, we learn that the two were childhood friends who shared a love of pulpy detective novels. (Harry's purple-prose narration of the film confirms his taste for overwritten tough-guy stories.) There's a murder and lots of chasing, but what you'll remember most about the movie is its oddball sense of humor and the very funny performances by its three leads.

Writer-director Shane Black obviously has a thing for Christmas, having also written *The Long Kiss Goodnight* and *Lethal Weapon* (see below), and *Kiss Kiss Bang Bang* gives us one of the sparkliest and most wonderfully artificial L.A. Christmases ever. (It's all the more impressive given that Black shot the film between February and May of 2004, which means the production had to provide its own fake trees and strings of lights.) Downey, Kilmer, and Monaghan—the latter looks quite fetching in her "sexy Santa" outfit, incidentally—maintain a perfect deadpan, no matter how absurd the situations or the dialogue become, and the result is a movie that doesn't spare the action or the laughs.

**FUN FACTS**
- Black on filming Christmas in Los Angeles: "Christmas appeals to me because it's promised magic, but in L.A. it's against the backdrop of something that's very sterile and something not full of goodwill. There's so little Christmas available, you sort of have to conjure it yourself. The magic is striving to break through. You have to really pay attention to find your Christmas, almost to earn it, which is what the characters have to do."
- A TV in the background of one scene is playing the loony Mexican kiddie movie *Santa Claus* (see p. 182).
- The film's chapters—"Lady in the Lake" (see below), "Trouble Is My Business," etc.—are all named after works by legendary Southern California–based detective novelist Raymond Chandler.
- Gay Perry's cell-phone ringtone is disco anthem "I Will Survive."

- The title of the film has a rich pedigree: It was a phrase often used on posters for James Bond movies in foreign countries in the 1960s; it's the title of film critic Pauline Kael's 1968 collection of essays; the original theme song to *Thunderball* (1965) was going to be a ditty called "Mr. Kiss Kiss Bang Bang," until producers decided that a hit single with the same title as the film made for better movie promotion, particularly on the heels of *Goldfinger* (1964).

## *Lady in the Lake* (1947)

**Unrated; 105 min. Written by Steven Fisher, based on the novel by Raymond Chandler. Directed by Robert Montgomery. Starring Robert Montgomery, Audrey Totter, Lloyd Nolan, Tom Tully. (Warner Home Video)**

Private eye Philip Marlowe (Montgomery) is hired by Adrienne Fromsett (Totter) to find Chrystal, the missing wife of her boss Derace Kingsby (Leon Ames). It's clear that Fromsett has romantic designs on Kingsby, but Marlowe flirts with her anyway. Marlowe's investigation brings him in contact with Chrystal's gigolo boyfriend Chris Lavery (Dick Simmons), several annoyed policemen, and a mystery woman (Jayne Meadows) who's somehow involved with several of the players. Marlowe, incidentally, appears in the film only in mirrors—the entire movie is presented from his point of view, with the camera taking his place and his voice heard from off-screen.

Once you get past the whole first-person gimmick of the movie, where all the characters speaking to Marlowe are acting directly toward the camera, *The Lady in the Lake* is a fun mystery, even if Chandler enthusiasts find it to be as scrubbed-up and nonsensical as most of the other adaptations of his novels during this period. Totter's a lot of fun to watch: Marlowe constantly catches Adrienne

Fromsett in a lie, leading her to switch from fake-smile to raised-eyebrow-grimace over and over again. In an introduction to the film—which features Montgomery's longest visible appearance—Marlowe tells us that we'll be shown all the clues to figure out the mystery for ourselves, but it's a whodunit almost as impenetrable as the legendarily unsolvable film version of Chandler's *The Big Sleep* (1946), which left even director Howard Hawks and his cast wondering who the killer was.

**FUN FACTS**

- Like many Christmas movies of the 1940s, *Lady in the Lake* features opening credits written on a series of Christmas cards. The difference here is that under the cards, there's a gun.
- Ames is perhaps best known as the father in the Christmas classic *Meet Me in St. Louis* (p. 205).
- *Lady in the Lake* is thought to be the first mainstream feature film in which the entire movie is told from the point of view of one character.
- This was the first film in which Montgomery—whose daughter Elizabeth would later star in the TV hit *Bewitched*—received billing as director; it was also his last film for MGM, where he'd been under contact for 18 years.
- Spoiler Alert: An actress named "Ellay Mort" is credited as playing Chrystal Kingsby; there's no such person. The name is a joke, since it's a phonetic translation of the French phrase "Elle est morte," i.e., "She's dead."

# *The Long Kiss Goodnight* (1996)

R; 120 min. Written by Shane Black. Directed by Renny Harlin. Starring Geena Davis, Samuel L. Jackson, Craig Bierko, Brian Cox. (New Line Home Video)

Samantha Caine (Davis) lives a seemingly idyllic existence as a schoolteacher and mom in a quaint small town in Pennsylvania. She doesn't realize that she's living a lie—Samantha is really Charly Baltimore, government assassin and all-around bad-ass, and ever since she suffered amnesia after almost being killed, she's actually inhabited one of her cover identities. After a car accident, her memories start returning to her, and with the help of shady private eye Mitch (Jackson), she's going to piece her life back together. But not if Timothy (Bierko), who tried to kill her the first time, can stop her first.

From a charming local parade (in which Samantha plays Mrs. Claus) to a heart-stopping, kick-out-the-jams final battle on a lit-up bridge between the United States and Canada, *The Long Kiss Goodnight* gets the most out of its Yuletide setting. And while it's often a supremely silly action movie, it's one of the few mainstream Hollywood films that allows a female protagonist to be as aggressive, violent, sexy, and deadly as her male counterparts. Jackson makes the most of his sidekick role, while Davis manages to be utterly convincing as both a Suzy Homemaker archetype and a ruthless killer. (When she tells a man who's torturing her, "Let me go now, and I'll leave you with the use of your legs," you believe her.)

See also: *Lethal Weapon* (1987), screenwriter Shane Black's other well-known Christmas action flick. From the shootout at the tree lot to bad guy Gary Busey firing a bullet into a TV showing the Alastair Sim version of *A Christmas Carol* (p. 147), the movie is steeped in the season. (The film even opens with "Jingle Bell Rock" and closes with "I'll Be Home for Christmas.") It's also the *Hamlet* of buddy-cop movies, the source of what would become a thousand clichés in the genre.

## *On Her Majesty's Secret Service* (1969)

**PG; 142 min. Written by Richard Maibaum, based on the novel by Ian Fleming. Directed by Peter Hunt. Starring George Lazenby, Diana Rigg, Telly Savalas, Gabriele Ferzetti. (MGM Home Video)**

James Bond 007 (Lazenby) falls for Contessa Teresa "Tracy" di Vicenzo (Rigg), whose father happens to be European crime lord Marc-Ange Draco (Ferzetti). Draco offers Bond a dowry of one million pounds to marry the troubled girl, which he refuses; Bond does offer to court her, however, if Draco will reveal the location of SPECTRE chief Ernst Stavro Blofeld (Savalas). Disguised as a genealogical expert, Bond visits Blofeld's fortress atop Piz Gloria in the Swiss Alps and discovers that Blofeld plans on turning a cadre of beautiful women from around the world into sleeper agents in a global germ warfare plot involving "Christmas presents" that actually carry deadly, crop-destroying spores.

The only James Bond Christmas movie to date comes sixth in the series, and it's a film that often gets short shrift because it's the only one to feature Lazenby as 007. Rigg ranks as one of the gutsiest and sexiest Bond girls, and the action sequences—including a chase through a Swiss holiday carnival—are some of the best in the series, leading some to surmise that, had Connery played the role, this would unquestionably be the ne plus ultra of the Bond films. But I agree with *Cult Films* author Danny Peary, who notes that Connery never would have pretended to be an asexual fop (complete with frilly shirt) the way that Lazenby does, nor would Bond's romance with Tracy—the one woman for whom he is willing to forsake all others—have played as tenderly with Connery's sadistic 007.

## FUN FACTS

- Lazenby wasn't the only one taking over a role from another actor—Blofeld had previously been played by Donald Pleasance in *You Only Live Twice* (1967). The villain would emerge again in *Diamonds Are Forever* (1971), this time played by Charles Gray, who would later teach us all to do the "Time Warp" in *The Rocky Horror Picture Show* (1975).

- This was the only film in the series to be directed by Hunt, who had been either a film editor or second unit director on the five previous 007 adventures.
- Arthouse fans may recognize Ferzetti from his role in Michelangelo Antonioni's *L'avventura*.
- It may not seem like much by today's standards, when most big Hollywood movies open on 2,000 or more screens in the United States alone, but *Majesty's* had one of the widest opening weekends of any movie up to that time, launching simultaneously in 1,500 cinemas worldwide.
- Fans of *Absolutely Fabulous* should be on the lookout for Joanna Lumley as one of Blofeld's beautiful "angels of death."

## *The Silent Partner* (1978)

R; 106 min. Written by Curtis Hanson, based on the novel *Think of a Number* by Anders Bodelsen. Directed by Daryl Duke. Starring Elliott Gould, Christopher Plummer, Susannah York, Céline Lomez. (Lionsgate Home Video)

Bank teller Miles (Gould) realizes that mall Santa Harry (Plummer) is casing the bank for a robbery, so Miles arranges for Harry to steal what amounts to pocket change from the drawers while Miles stashes the big bucks away for himself, knowing that Harry will be blamed for the missing money. Unfortunately for Miles, Harry knows what he's up to, and now he's forcing Miles to hand over the stolen loot. Can Miles outwit this dangerous criminal—as well as his bright and flirtatious co-worker Julie (York)—and get away with the perfect crime?

Despite its mundane trappings—a Toronto mall isn't exactly the Louvre—*The Silent Partner* ranks among the great heist movies, with crafty criminals staying multiple steps ahead of each other, as well as the audience, in planning their brilliant larceny. (Not for nothing does Miles read books about chess strategy.) Harry, commandingly portrayed by Plummer, makes for a frighteningly violent adversary to the soft-spoken and nerdy Miles, and the movie succeeds in making us wonder who's going to come out on top in their potentially deadly game of one-upmanship. Screenwriter Hanson (who would later write and direct 1997's *L.A. Confidential*) and director Duke build up agonizing suspense with plot devices like missing keys, inopportune phone calls, and other minor elements that could conceivably ruin Miles' scheme, and they brilliantly ratchet up the suspense toward a very tense and exciting climax. (There are some violent moments that make this one very much not for the kids.) It's a crafty caper movie that will keep you guessing until the very end.

**FUN FACTS**

- That's future *SCTV* and movie star John Candy as one of Miles' co-workers at the bank.
- *The Silent Partner* had an unsuccessful release in U.S. theaters, but after making several critics' Top 10 lists, another distributor gave the movie a second chance, resulting in its becoming a decent-sized hit.
- The U.S. Catholic Conference gave the film a "Condemned" rating for "cheap, corrosive cynicism that permeates it, together with the sex and violence."

# Three Days of the Condor (1975)

R; 117 min. Written by Lorenzo Semple Jr. and David Rayfiel, based on the novel *Six Days of the Condor* by James Grady. Directed by Sydney Pollack. Starring Robert Redford, Faye Dunaway, Cliff Robertson, Max von Sydow. (Paramount Home Video)

It's Christmastime in New York, and Joseph Turner (Redford) reports to work at what appears to be a pencil-pushing job at a literary society. This sedate office is secretly a division of the CIA, and Turner and his peers read books from all over the world, looking for hidden messages that revolutionaries and spies may be sending each other in plain sight. One day, while Turner is out picking up lunch, assassin Joubert (von Sydow) comes in and kills everyone in the office. A panicked Turner (code-named "Condor") calls his bosses for help, but when a CIA higher-up attempts to murder him at a rendezvous, Turner realizes he's on his own. The only person who can help him stay alive is Kathy (Dunaway), the initially terrified woman he's kidnapped who comes to believe his outlandish story.

The post-Watergate era was the perfect time for conspiracy thrillers wherein the government was as likely to kill you as protect you, and Sydney Pollack's *Three Days of the Condor* definitely ranks among the best of this suspenseful genre. Running for your life through the streets of New York City is terrifying enough; having to dodge Salvation Army bands playing "Good King Wenceslas" just adds to the tension of the situation. (There's also a darkly funny moment in a hospital where a radio plays "Joy to the World" as EKG machines provide a backbeat.) The "high-tech" devices that Redford and his fellow nerdy spies use may be horribly out-of-date, but the tension remains heart-stopping in this classic.

## FUN FACTS

- *The Simpsons* once parodied the film's title (but not its content) in an episode called "Three Gays of the Condo."
- When CIA higher-up Wabash (John Houseman) reminisces, "I sailed the Adriatic with a movie star at the helm," he's referring to actor Sterling Hayden, who served with the OSS (the predecessor to the CIA) running German blockades of the Adriatic to bring supplies to Yugoslav partisans.
- If the balcony of Higgins' (Robertson) office looks familiar, it's because it figures in the French documentary *9/11*, shot inside the

World Trade Center after the planes hit but before the buildings collapsed.

## Trapped in Paradise (1994)

**PG-13; 111 min. Written and directed by George Gallo. Starring Nicolas Cage, Jon Lovitz, Dana Carvey, Mädchen Amick. (20th Century Fox Home Entertainment)**

Scam-artist-turned-restaurant-manager Bill Firpo (Cage) has done his best to leave his life of crime behind him. When his brothers Dave (Lovitz) and Alvin (Carvey) get paroled at Christmastime because of prison overcrowding, however, Bill gets sucked into their plans to rob a barely guarded bank in the small town of Paradise, PA. The bank job itself is a piece of cake—getting out of town, however, proves to be tricky, what with a blizzard moving in. After the bank president, who doesn't know the Firpos are the one who robbed him, invites the boys to spend Christmas with his family, the thieves feel wracked with guilt. Complicating matters is Bill's attraction to bank teller Sarah (Amick), whose father happens to be the prisoner who originally came up with the notion to rob the bank—and who has broken out of jail to get revenge on the Firpos for stealing his idea.

The whole easy-robbery-impossible-escape farce idea was perhaps better executed by Bill Murray and Howard Franklin in 1990's *Quick Change*, but Gallo—as he did in *29th Street* (p. 82)—does a great job of mixing Noo Yawk brashness with holiday sentimentality. (Ma Firpo, as memorably played by Florence Stanley, is about as far from a doting, cookie-baking mom as you can imagine, but her every utterance is hysterically funny.) Cage operates in the put-upon, slow-burn mode he perfected in *Honeymoon in Vegas* (1992), and he hilariously juggles his moronic brothers, their half-baked robbery scheme, and the overly kind citizens of Paradise with aplomb.

Watching him take an entire diner hostage just to get the one bank employee with the key to the vault is a joy to behold.

**FUN FACTS**

- This was Gallo's second feature as writer-director, following *29th Street*. He was inspired to write the script after seeing a TV special in which criminals were reunited with their victims.
- During shooting in the Canadian town of Niagara-on-the-Lake, temperatures dropped to as low as 40 degrees below zero. Nonetheless, the production still had to import 75,000 pounds of biodegradable potato flakes (and half a dozen wind machines) for the blizzard sequences.
- *Trapped in Paradise* was one of the first films to include a closing credit stating, "No rainforest timber was used in the production of this motion picture," with the approval of the Rainforest Action Network.
- Bill Murray was originally cast as one of the Firpo brothers. Shooting titles for the film included *Home for the Holidays* and *It Happened in Paradise*.

# CHAPTER 6

Oliver MacGreevy terrorizes murderess Joan Collins in *Tales from the Crypt* (1972).

# There'll Be Scary Ghost Stories

## HOLIDAY HORROR

Christmas is the coziest of holidays, all about home and hearth and family and generosity and togetherness, with people coming together in kindness and understanding. So it was only a matter of time before someone figured out a way to make it terrifying.

Every other holiday on the calendar—from Halloween to Valentine's Day to April Fools' Day—has become fodder for masked killers, so why should Christmas be exempt? (The fourth Thursday in November remains a holdout, although Eli Roth promises to deliver on the mock trailer for *Thanksgiving* that he created for 2007's *Grindhouse*.) And if Dickens could work four ghosts into one of the best-loved Christmas stories of all time (Chapter 7), why not have some movies where bloodthirsty boogeymen—and other creatures who go bump in the night—go on a Yuletide rampage?

# Black Christmas (aka Silent Night, Evil Night) (1974)

R; 98 min. Written by Roy Moore. Directed by Bob Clark. Starring Olivia Hussey, Keir Dullea, Margot Kidder, John Saxon. (Somerville House)

A sorority house throws one last big blowout before everyone leaves for Christmas break, but the festivities are periodically interrupted by a series of grotesque and obscene phone calls from an unknown pervert. Everyone laughs off the calls, but then nice-girl Clare (Lynne Griffin) goes missing. As her sorority sisters search for her, the police try to trace the calls. Meanwhile, Jess (Hussey) tells her unstable musician boyfriend Peter (Dullea) that she wants to terminate her pregnancy; potty-mouthed Barb (Kidder) taunts the caller and gets sarcastic with the local police; and drunken house mother Mrs. Mac (Marion Waldman) staggers around the house looking for her hidden bottles of booze. Will any of these women find the heavy-breathing killer before it's too late?

John Carpenter's terrifying *Halloween* (1978) is often credited as a pioneering slasher film, but Bob Clark—who would later make a very different holiday classic with *A Christmas Story* (p. 199)—got there first with this chilling girls-in-peril thriller. (*Black Christmas* also created a terrific horror trope that would be stolen by a later movie, but to reveal it would be to spoil one of the film's best surprises.) Between the truly unsettling phone calls and the strong performances—Kidder in particular makes an impression as a cynical rich girl given to statements like "You can't rape a townie"—the suspenseful and disturbing *Black Christmas* delivers a bounty of shock and suspense to your stocking.

## FUN FACTS

- Ten months after its original release, *Black Christmas* ranked as the second highest-grossing feature film made in Canada, behind *The Apprenticeship of Duddy Kravitz*, released the same year.

Douglas McGrath, who plays the dim-witted sergeant, starred in *Goin' Down the Road* (1970), one of the first Canadian feature films to achieve international prominence.

- The film was retitled in the U.S. during its original release, according to producer Gerry Arbeid: "Warner Bros. executives wanted the title changed because they felt white audiences would stay away thinking *Black Christmas* was for blacks."

- Warner Bros. attempted to promote the film's New York opening with a toll-free phone number that people could call to get a "weird" message, akin to the movie's obscene phone calls. The gimmick worked so well—with 7,000 phone calls coming in over the course of one evening—that the studio's entire phone exchange was shut down, making incoming and outgoing calls impossible.

- *Black Christmas* was remade, badly, in 2006. They did at least have the smarts to cast Andrea Martin (one of the original film's sorority sisters) as the house mother, but otherwise—avoid.

## *Christmas Evil (aka You Better Watch Out)* (1980)

**Written and directed by Lewis Jackson. Starring Brandon Maggart, Jeffrey DeMunn, Dianne Hull. (Synapse Films and other sources)**

On Christmas Eve 1947, young Harry sees Mommy do more than just kiss Santa Claus; he's so shaken by the event that he smashes a Christmas snowglobe, cuts himself with the broken glass, and bleeds on the snowy cabin inside. Cut to 33 years later: Grown-up Harry (Maggart) sleeps in Santa Claus pajamas, covers his wall with St. Nick paraphernalia, creates a fake "Santa" beard with shaving cream, and monitors the neighborhood kids for his "naughty" and "nice" lists. He's cruelly exploited at his job at a toy factory and eventually snaps. Soon, Harry's expressing his rage—while dressed as Santa—by murdering people he perceives as "naughty" while setting up his own toy workshop at home. Adults track down

Harry, but children come to "Santa's" defense before he gets in his van and . . . well, you'll have to see for yourself.

Lewis Jackson's sole film as writer-director got a rave review from John Waters (*Female Trouble*, p. 37), who calls *Christmas Evil* "the best seasonal film of all time . . . If I had kids, I'd make them watch it every year, and if they didn't like it they'd be punished." (Waters later recorded a DVD commentary track for the film.) Unlike the later *Silent Night, Deadly Night* (see below), whose protagonist is obsessed with the whole punish-the-naughty part of the job, this movie gives us a maniacal Santa who balances his kind, gift-giving side with a stern sense of discipline. Creepy, funny, and unsettling, *Christmas Evil* ranks as a holiday horror must-see.

**FUN FACTS**

- Brandon Maggart later starred on the cable sitcom *Brothers* and is the father of singer Fiona Apple. (He also received a Tony nomination for the Broadway musical *Applause*.) *Home Improvement* star Patricia Richardson has an early role as one of the neighborhood moms.
- One of the cops is played by Raymond J. Barry, who got a promotion to chief of police in *The Ref* (p. 46); he's one of three cast members—along with Rutanya Alda and Bill Raymond—the two films share.
- One critic called the film's climax "a heartwarming sight for the mentally ill of all ages."
- Kathleen Turner auditioned for, but didn't land, the role of Harry's sister-in-law.

# *Gremlins* (1984)

PG; 106 min. Written by Chris Columbus. Directed by Joe Dante. Starring Zach Galligan, Phoebe Cates, Hoyt Axton, Polly Holliday. (Warner Home Video)

On a trip to New York City, unsuccessful inventor Rand Peltzer (Axton) searches for a Christmas present for his son Billy (Galligan), and in Chinatown he finds an adorable creature known as a mogwai. The old shopkeeper (Keye Luke) refuses to sell it, but his grandson secretly lets Rand have the animal for $300. There are rules to be followed in keeping the creature: Keep it out away from bright light, don't let it get wet, and don't feed it after midnight. Billy is delighted to receive the pet, whom he names Gizmo, but havoc erupts when the rules are ignored. Once he gets wet, Gizmo spawns several more mogwai, only these new ones are mean and aggressive. And when the new creatures eat after midnight, they go into cocoon stage, only to re-emerge as scaly, vicious creatures. The Peltzers and Billy's girlfriend Kate (Cates)—with the help of Gizmo—must save their town of Kingston Falls from the evil, vulgar, rampaging beasties.

Joe Dante has always had a mordant sense of humor, and getting to combine slimy creatures with an idyllic, snowy small town at Christmas time was a juxtaposition he clearly relished. Kingston Falls is a close cousin to the Bedford Falls of *It's a Wonderful Life* (p. 202)—there's even a mean old rich person to cause misery, although in this case, Mrs. Deagle (Holliday) comes to a much more violent end than Mr. Potter. The effects get rather splattery for a PG movie (see "Fun Facts," below) and Columbus' script has some hoary moments (all of which are brilliantly spoofed in the even funnier 1990 sequel, *Gremlins 2: The New Batch*), but *Gremlins* has a ghoulish sense of humor that makes it an annual must among people who look to Tim Burton (*The Nightmare Before Christmas*, p. 209), Edward Gorey, or Hieronymous Bosch rather than Currier & Ives for their holiday inspiration.

**FUN FACTS**

- The gore and violence of the PG-rated *Gremlins*, which came with a "Steven Spielberg Presents" seal of approval, was one of two movies in the summer of 1984 that inspired the Motion Picture

Association of America to create the PG-13 rating. (The other? Spielberg's *Indiana Jones and the Temple of Doom*.)

- Comedian and *Deal or No Deal* host Howie Mandel provided the voice of Gizmo.

- Dante loaded *Gremlins* with lots of film-nerd inside jokes, from the casting of Dick Miller and Jackie Joseph from the original *The Little Shop of Horrors* (1960) as the Futtermans to the brief appearance of Robby the Robot from *Forbidden Planet* (1956) at an inventors' convention to a cameo by Jim McKrell as newscaster Lew Landers, the role he played in Dante's *The Howling* (1981). The film also marks the final screen appearances of veteran character actors Scott Brady and Edward Andrews as, respectively, the local sheriff and Billy's boss.

- Some 50 companies paid for the rights to manufacture tie-in products, including paperback novelizations, children's records, lunch boxes, sleepwear, toys and dolls, air fresheners, pens, flashlights, masks, camping gear, videogames, watches and clocks, T-shirts and other clothing, beach towels, and greeting cards. Stickers were available to purchasers of Scott Tissues, Hi-C fruit drink, and Crest toothpaste. Oh, and Gremlins cereal, from Ralston Purina, of course. A company not officially tied into the film was Hasbro, which changed the look of its popular Furby doll to resemble Gizmo; the studio sued, and Hasbro settled for an undisclosed seven-figure sum.

- *Gremlins* features the first on-screen appearance of the logo for Spielberg's Amblin Entertainment company. It also marked the reappearance of the Warner Brothers "shield" logo after more than a decade of the abstract W logo designed by Saul Bass.

## *Jack Frost* (1997)

R; 89 min. Written by Michael Cooney; story by Jeremy Paige. Directed by Michael Cooney. Starring Scott MacDonald, Christopher Allport, Stephen Mendel, Shannon Elizabeth. (Allumination)

Murderer Jack Frost (MacDonald) is being transported to his execution. Taking advantage of the blinding snowstorm, he manages to overpower his captors, but not before the vehicle collides with a truck from a genetic research lab. The truck explodes, covering Frost in some sort of bizarre acid that makes his DNA merge with the snow on the ground in Snomonton, the Snowman Capital of the Midwest. By sheer coincidence, Snomonton's sheriff Sam (Allport) is the cop who sent Frost to prison, and now that the murderer is on the loose (and made of snow), he's out for vengeance. Sam had hoped that Frost's execution at midnight would put an end to his nightmares, but now the lawman finds that he's got to capture this crazed killer all over again. Can this deadly snowman be apprehended before he murders the entire town?

OK, yes, the premise of a homicidal snowman is ridiculous, but *Jack Frost* knows it, keeping tongue firmly in cheek as its frosty killer strings up people with Christmas lights and assaults the nubile Shannon Elizabeth (in her screen debut, three years before her breakout role in 1999's *American Pie*) in a bathtub. The cast manages to keep a straight face for this silliest of horror-movie premises, and writer-director Cooney keeps the violent mayhem coming while creating some entertaining tension between Sam and the visiting federal agents and scientists who try to take over the investigation. (True to horror-movie form, the interlopers from out of town fail to be of any help whatsoever). It's the perfect movie to have on in the background of a Christmas party—assuming your friends are of the right temperament, of course—so that people will periodically come up and ask, "Um . . . is this a movie about a snowman killing people at Christmastime?" Oddly enough, this film manages to be less disturbing than the sappy Michael Keaton flick of the same name, in which a dead dad remains in his kid's life by reincarnating himself as a snowman. One *Jack Frost* horrifies on purpose; the other one does it by accident.

**FUN FACTS**

- In case anyone was unclear on the basic plot of the movie, the sequel—*Jack Frost 2: Revenge of the Mutant Killer Snowman* (2000)—spells it all out right there in the title.
- The closing credits include the line "All Credit Cards Provided By: The Director."

# *Night of the Hunter* (1955)

**Unrated; 95 min. Written by James Agee, based on the novel by Davis Grubb. Directed by Charles Laughton. Starring Robert Mitchum, Lillian Gish, Shelley Winters, Billy Chapin. (MGM Home Video)**

Harry Powell (Mitchum) claims to be a preacher, but he's a twisted murderer who has married a string of women only to murder them for their money. Powell shares a jail cell with Ben Harper (Peter Graves), who is sentenced to death for killing two policemen during the robbery of $10,000, which authorities never recovered. Powell marries Harper's widow Willa (Winters), hoping to find the money, and makes her feel guilty for even thinking about expecting marital relations with him. He pretends not to care about the stolen loot, but Willa catches him trying to force her son John (Chapin) to reveal its whereabouts. After Harper murders Willa—leaving her body underwater, where her blonde hair drifts with the reeds—John and his baby sister Pearl (Sally Jane Bruce) run away. They are eventually taken in by no-nonsense widow Mrs. Cooper (Gish), who may be their only protection against the dastardly Powell.

No matter how many times you watch *Night of the Hunter*, you'll be terrified by Mitchum's unsettling performance. From his hands—famously tattooed with the words LOVE and HATE—to his ability to go from fake-spiritual to nakedly evil, Harry Powell is a fearsome creation. The opening sequence features Mrs. Cooper telling a story to a group of children, so it's not surprising that the film has the qualities of both a fable and a dream, particularly the expressionistic sequence, beautifully shot by legendary cinematographer Stanley Cortez, in which fugitives John and Pearl drift down the river toward what they hope is safety. (The film's memorable Christmas climax acts as a perfect coda to the film's battles between good and evil.) Laughton never directed another feature, but his one stint behind the camera nonetheless ranks as one of the most eccentric and entertainingly disturbing films ever made.

**FUN FACTS**

- Laughton didn't particularly like children, so Mitchum wound up directing the performances of his young co-stars.
- Laughton convinced Gish, one of the giants of the silent screen, to come out of semi-retirement for the film.
- A rumor persisted for years that Laughton threw out Agee's script and rewrote the entire film, but recent research indicates that Laughton merely prevailed upon Agee to trim his very long first draft to a more manageable length.

## *Silent Night, Bloody Night* (1974)

R; 81 min. Written by Theodore Gershuny, Jeffrey Konvitz, and Ira Teller; story by Konvitz and Teller. Directed by Theodore Gershuny. Starring Patrick O'Neal, Mary Woronov, John Carradine, James Patterson. (Alpha Video and other sources)

Diane (Woronov) stands outside the foreboding Butler House in her small village and reflects upon the events of the previous Christmas Eve. Big-city lawyer John Carter (O'Neal) had come to the village to sell the house on behalf of his client Jeffrey Butler (Patterson), who inherited the place upon the death of his grandfather. But that same day, an inmate at an asylum for the criminally insane escaped and made his way to Butler House. Over the course of the evening, long-buried secrets would be revealed, and many of the people in-volved with Butler House's dark history would find themselves fac-ing an ax-wielding lunatic.

Despite its lurid title and evident low budget, *Silent Night, Bloody Night* is a chilling and atmospheric little fright flick. The story doesn't entirely make sense upon first viewing, but the standout cast is so committed to the goings-on that it doesn't really matter; even if the plot's ultimate revelations aren't completely logical, there are enough solid scares and a general sense of underlying dread that make the movie supremely effective. (There's an extended sepia-toned flash-back that's way more visually interesting than what you might expect from an early 1970s B-movie.) There are hints of slasher-style shocks here, but overall, it's a film that's more interested in creeping up on you and lingering in your psyche long after you've finished watching it.

## FUN FACTS

- Woronov—who was married to director Gershuny at the time—was a veteran of the Andy Warhol "factory" of the 1960s, having appeared in *Chelsea Girls* (1966) and other Warhol projects. She apparently dug out her Rolodex to help cast the film: Other mem-bers of the Warhol ensemble who appear in *Silent Night, Bloody Night* include Candy Darling, Ondine, Jack Smith (director of the 1963 underground classic *Flaming Creatures*), Susan Rothenberg (who went on to become an acclaimed contemporary painter), Kristen Steen, Tally Brown, and Lewis Love.
- Veteran actor John Carradine does not speak in the film—his one line of "croaked" dialogue was later dubbed.
- Lloyd Kaufman, the low-budget impresario behind Troma Films, received one of his first credits as Associate Producer on *Silent Night, Bloody Night*.
- Despite what the film's ending implies, the house used as the film's principal location still stands on Long Island, in the city of Oyster Bay.

# Silent Night, Deadly Night (1984)

R; 85 min. Written by Michael Hickey; story by Paul Caimi. Directed by Charles E. Sellier Jr. Starring Robert Brian Wilson, Linnea Quigley, Jeff Hansen, Charles Dierkop. (Anchor Bay Entertainment)

In 1971, young Billy (Jonathan Best) has the worst Christmas Eve ever. First his insane grandfather (Will Hare) tells him that Santa punishes wicked children—"You see Santy Claus tonight, you better run, boy! You better run for your life!"—and then, as Billy's family returns home, a thief in a Santa costume shoots Billy's dad and then rapes and murders his mother. Billy goes to live in an orphanage, where the humorless Mother Superior (Lilyan Chauvin) refuses to coddle the boy's terror about Santa Claus, forcing the lad to sit on St. Nick's lap. (Billy punches the guy and runs off.) Cut to 1984, where a grown-up Billy (Wilson) gets a job at a toy store. He's the ideal employee—until Christmas rolls around and he's forced to dress up as Santa. After having kids on his lap all day (he warns them that Santa will get them if they're bad), Billy finally snaps and wreaks bloody vengeance upon the naughty.

Silent Night, Deadly Night is most (in)famous for the hue and cry it elicited upon its original release: Parents' groups around the country decried the fact that Santa Claus had been turned into a slasher, and film critics Gene Siskel and Roger Ebert actually read the names of the writers, director, and producers on their TV show, saying "Shame!" after each one. Christmas Evil opened years earlier, but since Silent Night, Deadly Night was released by a major studio (Columbia Pictures' TriStar Pictures division), it naturally got more attention. When all is said and done and the controversy is put aside, however, this is a competent and occasionally chilling little horror tale. It's shameless in its devotion to slasher-movie tropes—women constantly shed their tops, a horny babysitter and her half-naked boyfriend get gruesomely murdered, and the ending perfectly sets up a sequel—but the filmmakers at least throw in a macabre Christmas carol called "Santa's Watching" that underlines the idea of Father Christmas as a terrifying figure who sneaks into your house every December 24.

**FUN FACTS**
- Original distributor TriStar reacted to the controversy by dropping the film after one week in release. Aquarius Releasing picked it up and used the brouhaha as a selling point: "The Movie That Went Too Far! . . . that so outraged Hollywood, the Government and parents everywhere. They Tried to Ban It! . . . the movie so shocking, so disturbing They Didn't Want You to See It! Now You Can See It . . . Uncut . . . in all its terrifying horror."
- One notable protestor against the film was actor Mickey Rooney, who said, "How dare they! I'm all for the First Amendment, but . . . don't give me Santa Claus with a gun going to kill someone. The scum who made that movie should be run out of town." (Here's a general rule of thumb: When someone says, "I'm all for the First Amendment, but . . . " they're not all for the First Amendment.) Rooney clearly got over his digust, as he agreed to star as "Joe Petto" in the direct-to-video sequel *Silent Night, Deadly Night 5: The Toy Maker* (1991).
- Billy's workplace, "Ira's Toys," was named for the film's producer, Ira Richard Barmak.
- Director Sellier had previously written such cheesy documentaries as *In Search of Noah's Ark* (1976) and *The Lincoln Conspiracy* (1977).
- Either all the Santa suits in *Silent Night, Deadly Night* had the same jingle bells sewn into the cuff . . . or the movie uses just one Santa suit over and over again.

## *Tales From the Crypt* (1972)

PG; 92 min. Written by Milton Subotsky, based on EC Comics stories by Johnny Craig, Al Feldstein, and William M. Gaines. Directed by Freddie Francis. Starring Joan Collins, Chloe Franks, Martin Boddey, Oliver MacGreevy. (20th Century Fox Home Entertainment)

A group of British tourists visiting ancient catacombs are diverted from their group by a mysterious crypt-keeper (Sir Ralph Richardson), who tells them horrifying stories about dastardly deeds that they intend to commit—or have they already committed them? In the first tale in this horror anthology, ". . . All Through the House," Joanne (Collins) murders her rich husband (Boddey) on Christmas Eve. While she's trying to dispose of the body, she has to keep her young daughter (Franks)—excited about Santa's imminent arrival—from getting out of bed. Meanwhile, a murderous lunatic in a Santa Claus costume has escaped from the local insane asylum and is lurking around Joanne's house. Don't you just hate it when you want to call the police, but can't because you're trying to get rid of a corpse?

Collins turns out to be quite the scream queen in this British homage to vintage American horror comics. (George Romero and Stephen King would later create *Creepshow* [1982], their own salute to the skin-crawlingly hilarious horror titles from EC Comics.) ". . . All Through the House" has its own O. Henry–style twist, making it a nifty little holiday horror tale for people who would have liked "Gift of the Magi" better had there been a serial killer in it. (The other *Tales*, while not set at Christmas, are equally chilling.)

### FUN FACTS

- The vignettes in *Tales From the Crypt* were based on stories from the 1950s horror comics *Tales From the Crypt* and *The Vault of*

*Horror*. (The original ". . . All Through the House" story appeared in *The Vault of Horror* #35.) These titles, as well as other popular EC Comics publications like *The Haunt of Fear* and *Shock Suspen-Stories*, were taken off the market in the mid-1950s after they were vilified in a Congressional hearing on juvenile delinquency and in Fredric Wertham's controversial book *Seduction of the Innocent*. The comics nonetheless went on to influence generations of horror writers and fans, and they are now available in handsomely mounted hardback editions.

- *Tales From the Crypt* was later revived as an HBO series; the second episode was an adaptation of ". . . All Through the House" directed by Robert Zemeckis.
- The "killer Santa Claus" horror sub-genre is believed to have started with this film.

## Whoever Slew Auntie Roo? (aka *Who Slew Auntie Roo?*) (1971)

PG; 91 min. Written by Robert Blees and Jimmy Sangster; additional dialogue by Gavin Lambert; story by David D. Osborn. Directed by Curtis Harrington. Starring Shelley Winters, Mark Lester, Chloe Franks, Sir Ralph Richardson. (MGM Home Video)

Mrs. Robin Forrest (Winters) is a wealthy and mentally unhinged widow who keeps the corpse of her dead daughter Catherine in the upstairs nursery. Every year, Mrs. Forrest invites a group of children from the local orphanage to spend Christmas at her lavish estate, Forrest Grange; usually, the orphanage chooses only the best-behaved children to go, but perpetual runaways Christopher (Lester) and Katy (Franks) stow away in the trunk of the car transporting the orphans. Mrs. Forrest invites them to stay. That night, during one of her regular séances attempting to reach Catherine, Katy wanders into the room, making Mrs. Forrest believe that her child has been reincarnated. After Christmas, when the other children leave, Katy has been secretly locked inside the nursery. Christopher escapes to find her, and upon returning to Forrest Grange, he believes that he and Katy—like Hansel and Gretel before them—must destroy the strange old lady before she eats them up.

While the film lays on the "Hansel and Gretel" references with a thick trowel—as if the audience wasn't going to pick up on the parallels—*Whoever Slew Auntie Roo?* is an engagingly ghoulish tale which, like the fable that inspired it, follows two helpless children as they battle seemingly indomitable forces. Winters has a ball playing the nutty old woman—she terrifies Christopher with the way she eats an apple, marking a rare occasion when an actress is *literally* chewing the scenery—and the 1920s-set film is steeped in eerie atmosphere. If you've got kids who enjoy being scared and aren't prone to nightmares, this is a macabre Christmas tale they can sink their teeth into.

**FUN FACTS**

- Director Harrington knew his way around a séance—he was known for being an active member in the Los Angeles occult scene. Harrington also came up through the avant-garde film movement—having collaborated on some of the early films of Kenneth Anger—and spearheaded the movement to restore James Whale's horror classic *The Old Dark House* (1932). A friend of Whale's late in the legendary director's life, Harrington provided guidance (and a cameo appearance) to Bill Condon's film about Whale, *Gods and Monsters* (1998).

- *Whoever Slew Auntie Roo?* is considered to be part of a horror sub-genre known as "psycho-biddy," wherein aging Hollywood actresses played off their one-time glamour by playing terrifying (or terrified) women in horror films. This style of horror movie launched with, depending on whom you ask, either *Sunset Blvd.* (1950) or *What Ever Happened to Baby Jane?* (1962), and also included *Hush . . . Hush, Sweet Charlotte* (1964), *Picture Mommy Dead* (1966), *What Ever Happened to Aunt Alice?* (1969), and another Winters-Harrington collaboration, *What's the Matter With Helen?* (1971). Psycho-biddy films also came to be known as "hagsploitation" or "Grande Dame Guignol."

- Actress Judy Cornwell, who plays Winters' maid in the film—and would later appear as Mrs. Claus in the dreadful *Santa Claus: The Movie* (p. 186)—wrote in her memoirs years later that, after Winters found out that Cornwell had gotten rave reviews for her performance in *Wuthering Heights* (1970), the two-time Oscar winner demanded that the young British actress' role be cut down to nearly nothing.

- Yes, that's gooiest-Tiny-Tim-ever Richard Beaumont (p. 151) from the 1970 *Scrooge* as one of the orphans. And Santa only knows if Chloe Franks became forever traumatized about Christmas after shooting this and *Tales From the Crypt* (p. 137) back-to-back.

# CHAPTER 7

Mister Magoo, as Scrooge, buys the biggest turkey in the window in *Mister Magoo's Christmas Carol* (1962).

# Scrooge-a-Palooza
## 'A CHRISTMAS CAROL' ON FILM

Since its publication in 1843, *A Christmas Carol* has become part of the holiday's collective DNA. From local theater productions (many dramatic societies perform the Charles Dickens classic every year as a reliable money-earner) to sitcom spoof versions to the many film adaptations, this story of the greedy, selfish, and miserly Ebenezer Scrooge—and how four ghosts teach him to love life, the less fortunate, and Christmas—is one we've all seen again and again. It is perhaps the ultimate tale of redemption, which is what makes it such a perfect Christmastime story.

Spoiler alert (for a 160+-year-old story): Much of this chapter assumes the reader already knows the story of Ebenezer Scrooge and how it all turns out. If you want to avoid too many plot spoilers, skip down to the "Rating" section for each film, and definitely skip the next few paragraphs.

Most of us know the tale by heart, but here it is in a nutshell: The greediest, most miserly, most pinched man in Victorian London is Ebenezer Scrooge, who loathes Christmas and pretty much everyone and everything else. On the night of Christmas Eve, the ghost of his former business partner, Jacob Marley, appears to Scrooge on the seventh anniversary of his death wrapped up in heavy chains, a punishment for thinking more about money than about mankind while he lived. Marley hopes to spare Scrooge the same fate and warns his old friend that three more ghosts will visit him.

The Spirit of Christmas Past takes Scrooge to his lonely childhood as a schoolboy and shows him the year his sister Fan rescued him from school and brought him back home. Scrooge sees his kindly old boss Mr. Fezziwig, who hosted a lively Christmas party; he also sees Belle, the woman he loved but who eventually left him because he loved money more than he loved her. (Some of the films refer to her as "Isabel" or some alternate spelling thereof.) The spirit also shows Belle in the present, surrounded by adoring children that might have been Scrooge's.

The Spirit of Christmas Present, a robust bearded man in a green robe and carrying a horn of plenty, showers goodwill on people everywhere. He shows Scrooge the modest but loving celebrations at the home of Scrooge's underpaid clerk, Bob Cratchit, whose youngest son Tiny Tim is very sick and may die without proper medical attention. Scrooge also sees the lively dinner at the house of his nephew Fred (the son of Fan, who died in childbirth), whose invitation he turns down every year, despite the fact that Fred is Scrooge's only living relative.

The eerie Spirit of Christmas Yet to Come shows Scrooge that his death moves no one, because he has no friends. Business associates say they'll attend his funeral only if there's a free lunch; Scrooge's maid, laundress, and undertaker sell his personal belongings at a junk shop; Tiny Tim dies; and Scrooge is buried, unloved, in a poorly tended grave.

Scrooge awakes as a new man, determined to hold Christmas dear and to open his heart. And thanks to all these film versions, you can watch Scrooge's transformation again and again and again:

(Note: While both *An American Carol* [2008] and *Ghosts of Girl-friends Past* [2009] borrow elements from the story, neither is set at Christmas and thus are not discussed here.)

## THE TRADITIONAL ADAPTATIONS

## *Scrooge* (1935)

Unrated; 63 min. (There also exists a 78 min. version.) Written by H. Fowler Mear. Directed by Henry Edwards. (Legend Films and other sources)

SETTING: In a London where the street-corner musicians don't necessarily play on key.

SCROOGE: Seymour Hicks, who had previously played the skinflint in a British silent in 1913; when young carolers gather at his window, his Scrooge's first instinct is to grab a stick.

CRATCHIT: An older gent (Donald Calthrop) than usual, but still believable as a parent.

MARLEY: Invisible! And the voice: Uncredited!

GHOST 2: Marie Ney plays the Ghost of Christmas Past as a blurry spectre.

GHOST 3: This Spirit of Christmas Present (Oscar Asche) is clean-shaven, but works the classic robe and head wreath. The ghost calls back Scrooge's line about how "the surplus population" ought to die, but in the 63-minute edit, Scrooge hasn't said it.

TINY TIM: Philip Frost is one of the screen's youngest in this role; Scrooge gets to say Tim's famous "God bless us, every one" line, making this Tiny Tim a touch less treacly than usual.

GHOST 4: Just the ominous shadow of a pointing hand—which is really all you need.

MEMORABLE DIALOGUE: Scrooge, watching the Cratchits celebrate Christmas, "Laugh [at them]? I envy them!"

RATING: Very early-talkie in its scratchy audio and relative lack of camera movement. (And what the Lord Mayor of London and a rousing chorus of "God Save the Queen" have to do with A Christmas Carol remains a mystery.)

## A Christmas Carol (1938)

**Unrated; 69 min. Written by Hugo Butler. Directed by Edwin L. Marin. (Warner Home Video)**

SETTING: As the film's opening title proclaims, "More Than a Century Ago . . . in London . . . on Christmas Eve."

SCROOGE: Reginald Owen as an old man crabby enough to suck the life out of the room when Fred and Bob try to have a Christmas toast.

CRATCHIT: Gene Lockhart, one of the great comedic second bananas of the '30s. (How did he get so plump on Scrooge's miserable wages?) Scrooge fires him after he accidentally knocks his boss' hat off in the street with a snowball.

MARLEY: The always formidable Leo G. Carroll; Scrooge tries calling the cops on this interloper, but of course, they see nothing.

GHOST 2: A glamorous blonde Spirit of Christmas Past (MGM contract player Ann Rutherford).

GHOST 3: Lionel Braham as the Spirit of Christmas Present. Beard, wreath, horn, robe, the usual.

TINY TIM: Introduced at the very beginning—he (Terry Kilburn) encounters Fred on his way to Scrooge's office. No sappier than your average juvenile performance of the time.

GHOST 4: The Spirit of Christmas Future, a hooded figure (D'Arcy Corrigan) on a bleak, windy plain.

MEMORABLE DIALOGUE: "Yes! Yes, I do! I like Christmas! I *love* Christmas!"

RATING: Straightforward and heartwarming—and at a brisk 69 minutes, good for viewers with short attention spans.

## *A Christmas Carol* (U.S.)/*Scrooge* (UK) (1951)

**Unrated; 86 min. Written by Noel Langley. Directed by Brian Desmond-Hurst. (VCI Entertainment)**

SCROOGE: Alastair Sim as the unkindest man at the London Exchange

CRATCHIT: Mervyn Johns. (Fun fact: Hermione Baddeley, who plays Mrs. Cratchit, is known to 1970s TV fans as Mrs. Naugatuck on *Maude*.)

MARLEY: Michael Hordern makes the ghost of Scrooge's old partner drily superior.

GHOST 2: The Spirit of Christmas Past (Michael Dolan) appears as a gentleman with long white hair in a flower-trimmed robe. This version strays a bit from the original by having young Scrooge and Marley (Patrick Macnee, future star of TV's *The Avengers*) drive Fezziwig out of business. Scrooge refuses to visit Marley's deathbed until after the end of the business day; a dying Marley tells Scrooge, "We were wrong. Save yourself!" Scrooge feels no sadness at his passing.

GHOST 3: The Spirit of Christmas Present (Francis de Wolff). Scrooge thinks he is too old for redemption; the spirit thinks otherwise.

TINY TIM: Less saccharine than most, as played by Glyn Dearman. Even his "God bless us, every one" goes down fairly easy.

GHOST 4: A cloaked being (C. Konarski), whose hands are covered in flesh and aren't the usual skeletal appendages. (You can see the actor's face through the Cratchits' window. Oops!) That's Ernest Thesiger from *The Old Dark House* (1932) and *Bride of Frankenstein* (1935) as the undertaker.

MEMORABLE DIALOGUE: Scrooge, after being told that Marley hasn't long to live: "Well, what do you want me to do about it? If he's dying, he's dying."

RATING: For many, this is their preferred *Christmas Carol* movie. Sim makes a great Scrooge, and the film is, on the whole, well acted, breezily paced, and its departures from Dickens' story are smartly crafted. (The film's editor was Clive Donner, who would go on to direct the 1984 TV movie.)

## *A Christmas Carol* (1984)

**Unrated; 100 min. Written by Roger O. Hirson. Directed by Clive Donner. (20th Century Fox Home Entertainment)**

SETTING: A dark, foggy, and gloomy Victorian London; even when it's not a ghost story, this is no scrubbed-up version of the past.

SCROOGE: A humorless, no-nonsense commodities broker (George C. Scott). He looks a lot like the John Leech illustrations that were originally published with the Dickens story (whereas Fred and several other characters have poofy hair of the '80s variety) and cackles when he bad-mouths Christmas. His "Bah!" is awesome, too.

CRATCHIT: David Warner. Odd to see this actor who specializes in villains playing such a meek and kind-hearted character, but he's fine in the role.

MARLEY: Frank Finlay—very heavy chains, removes his head wrap so that his unhinged jaw drops before he speaks. His gray pallor and milky contact lenses are impressive, and he seems genuinely racked with regret.

GHOST 2: Ghost of Christmas Past (Angela Pleasance), who carries the candle-snuffing cap referred to by Dickens.

GHOST 3: Edward Woodward, in the usual getup. (Says the ghost to Scrooge, "You mustn't argue with those we visit. It's pointless, and even tactless.")

TINY TIM: Actually meets Scrooge face-to-face on the 24th. As usual, Tim (Anthony Walters) is quite a drip; this one's more than a little creepy, too. He also looks at the camera more than once.

GHOST 4: Hooded, floating wraith in a fog bank, played by Michael Carter.

MEMORABLE DIALOGUE: "'Almost' carries no weight, especially in matters of the heart. And you did have a heart, didn't you, Ebenezer? Why didn't you follow her?"

RATING: Scott ranks among the great Scrooges, quietly threatening where other performers shout. He leads a fine cast of British actors that make this made-for-TV production a *Christmas Carol* to remember. A few cheesy special effects, but overall a top-drawer adaptation.

## A Christmas Carol (1999)

**Unrated; 95 min. Written by Peter Barnes. Directed by David Jones. (Turner Home Entertainment)**

SETTING: A dank, but festive, Victorian London.

SCROOGE: Patrick Stewart—he's not a wrinkly Scrooge, but he's unpleasant all the same. Another stick-grabber when kids come around to sing carols. (Stewart had originally performed *A Christmas Carol* as a one-man show and then expanded it into this made-for-cable movie.)

CRATCHIT: Richard E. Grant—an interesting choice that pays off.

MARLEY: Bernard Lloyd with chains and headwrap (he too does that off-putting dead-guy-with-agape-jaw thing). He first appears in etchings on Scrooge's wall; this is supposedly the first version to use digital effects.

GHOST 1: Joel Grey as a bright, androgynous candle, aka the Ghost of Christmas Past.

GHOST 2: Desmond Barrit, dressed in the usual Ghost of Christmas Present manner.

TINY TIM: Ben Tibber, not the worst. And Saskia Reeves (with unflattering eyebrows) as Mrs. Cratchit.

GHOST 3: Two dots of light within a hooded cloak. Scrooge falls into his own grave and lands facing his own corpse.

MEMORABLE DIALOGUE: Scrooge, after Cratchit asks if they should remove Mr. Marley's name from the sign outside: "No. Time will erase it at no cost to us."

RATING: Gets better as it goes along, although it could use some trimming. Overall, it's well cast and mostly fun to watch.


## THE MUSICALS

## *Mister Magoo's Christmas Carol* (1962)

Unrated; 53 min. Written by Barbara Chain. Directed by Abe Levitow. (Classic Media)

SETTING: A Broadway musical adaptation of the Dickens classic.

SCROOGE: Severely myopic Quincy Magoo (Jim Backus), playing Scrooge on stage.

MARLEY: Voiced by Royal Dano

GHOST 2: The sequence of events is somewhat scrambled—the Ghost of Christmas Present, complete with horn/torch and robe (and voiced by Les Tremayne) appears before the Ghost of Christmas Past. The Cratchits sing a somewhat depressing Christmas song about dreaming of better times and enjoying the little things for now.

TINY TIM: Gerald McBoingboing, star of the Oscar-winning short film of the same name. (In a series of animated shorts, Gerald spoke only in sound effects. *Mister Magoo's Christmas Carol* marked the first time the character uttered dialogue.) Oddly enough, this Tiny Tim, who also happens to be obsessed with something called "razzleberry dressing," is probably the most entertaining one of them all.

GHOST 3: The Ghost of Christmas Past, who appears as an androgynous boy (voiced by Joan Gardner, who also voices Tiny Tim) with a flame over his head. Young Scrooge sings a sad song about being alone; later, Fezziwig's daughter sings another sad song, about how Scrooge doesn't love her anymore.

GHOST 4: The Ghost of Christmas Yet to Come, a bony-handed hooded spectre. The laundress, maid, and undertaker take Scrooge's possessions to the junk dealer and sing a rollicking tune about being despicable.

MEMORABLE DIALOGUE: "You're the one who's too tight with a penny to buy himself a pair of spectacles."

RATING: The kind-hearted Magoo character winds up playing mean old Scrooge quite effectively, and this is a breezy version that kids should definitely enjoy. The mostly melancholy songs are written by Broadway legend Jule Styne, who composed the music for *Gypsy, Funny Girl,* and *Gentlemen Prefer Blondes,* among many others.

## *Scrooge* (1970)

**G; 113 min. Written by Leslie Bricusse. Directed by Ronald Neame. (Paramount Home Video)**

SETTING: A vividly realistic Victorian London where people none-theless are given to singing and dancing down the street en masse.

SCROOGE: This time, he's a penny-pinching moneylender (Albert Finney) and not someone whose trade is involved with the London Exchange. He describes himself well with the song "I Hate People."

CRATCHIT: The very charming David Collings.

MARLEY: Alec Guinness as a somewhat fey Marley, possessed of a dry and morbid sense of humor. Talks his way through his one song, Rex Harrison–style.

GHOST 2: Dame Edith Evans, in a lush red gown, as the Ghost of Christmas Past. Isobel (Suzanne Neve) gets a lovely song called "Happiness," which makes her eventual rejection of Scrooge all the more heartbreaking.

GHOST 3: Kenneth More, looking more like the original John Leech etching of the character than any of his counterparts. His song with Scrooge, "I Like Life," is so unabashedly joyous that it always brings tears to my eyes.

TINY TIM: Naturally, the score's one nails-on-chalkboard song, "The Beautiful Day," goes to Tiny Tim (Richard Beaumont).

GHOST 4: A cloaked, skeletal figure. The film's Oscar-nominated (and most famous) tune, "Thank You Very Much," is sung by the people who used to be in debt to Scrooge, who are serenading his casket. In this version, Marley greets Scrooge in hell, where he is put to work in a freezing cold office as Satan's clerk. Huge chains are brought out to wrap Scrooge up—before he awakens in his own bed, tangled in the sheets.

MEMORABLE DIALOGUE: "There is never enough time to do or say all the things that we would wish. The thing is to try to do as much as you can in the time that you have. Remember Scrooge, time is short, and suddenly, you're not there any more."

RATING: Even though this is a very post-*Oliver!* (1968) musical, with the streets of London packed with choreographed Cockneys, it's my favorite adaptation of *A Christmas Carol*, brimming with exuberance and boasting a wonderful performance by Finney playing Scrooge as both an old skinflint and a young man in love. It's totally understandable that, for many people, their favorite *Christmas Carol* movie is whichever one imprinted on them first; now that I've watched all of them—and incidentally, I saw *Scrooge* for the first time as an adult—I feel clear-eyed in saying that this is my pick of the lot.

## *The Muppet Christmas Carol* (1992)

G; 89 min. Written by Jerry Juhl. Directed by Brian Henson. (Walt Disney Home Entertainment)

SETTING: A Victorian England where humans and Muppets mingle freely.

SCROOGE: A shrewd and cruel moneylender played by Michael Caine.

CRATCHIT: Kermit the Frog (voiced by Steve Whitmire), with Miss Piggy (Frank Oz) as his wife. Oh, and Gonzo (Dave Goelz) as Charles Dickens, who narrates using the original text. Cratchit is aided in the office by a team of bookkeeping rats. The charitable fundraisers are played by Bunsen Honeydew (Goelz) and Beaker (Whitmire).

MARLEY: Statler (Jerry Nelson) and Waldorf (Goelz) as Jacob and Robert Marley, Scrooge's former partners, who constantly heckled him. (When Scrooge says Dickens' line about "more of gravy than the grave about you," they tell him what a terrible pun that is. "Leave the comedy to the bears, Ebenezer!") The moneyboxes on their spectral chains sing backup to their musical number.

GHOST 2: A floating child, voiced by Karen Prell. There's a headmaster played by Sam the Eagle (Oz). Then the Christmas dance hosted by—wait for it—Fozziewig (Oz as Fozzie Bear), owner of a rubber-chicken factory. Music provided by Dr. Teeth and the

Electric Mayhem, of course, and the Marleys are there to heckle Fozziewig.

GHOST 3: The usual bearded giant, but a Muppet version (voiced by Nelson). He ages over the course of his time on Earth, as in the original story.

TINY TIM: Played by Kermit's nephew Robin (voiced by Nelson). (The Cratchit boys are all frogs, the daughters are pigs.) Sings a goopy song.

GHOST 3: Hooded spectre; hands are ashen but not skeletal. Even Gonzo and Rizzo the Rat (who's been co-narrating; voiced by Whitmire) are too scared to follow along.

MEMORABLE DIALOGUE: "Christmas is a very busy time for us, Mr. Cratchit. People preparing feasts, giving parties, spending the mortgage money on frivolities. One might say that December is the foreclosure season. Harvest time for the moneylenders."

RATING: Caine is terrific, and the Muppets' unique brand of anarchic humor is very much on display. Sadly, the Paul Williams songs aren't as memorable as the ones he composed for *The Muppet Movie* (1979)—as my friend, film critic Curt Holman, once observed, too many of the tunes seems to build up to "la la la la *Chriiiiiiiist-maaaaaaaas!*"

## *A Christmas Carol: The Musical* (2004)

**Unrated; 97 min. Written by Lynn Ahrens. Directed by Arthur Allan Seidelman. (Lionsgate Home Entertainment)**

SETTING: A Victorian London that is somehow simultaneously snowy and sunny.

SCROOGE: An irascible broker (Kelsey Grammer) who's legendary as the meanest man in the London Exchange.

CRATCHIT: Edward Gower; unlike most other Bob Cratchits, this one actually tries talking to Scrooge about Tiny Tim and his troubles.

MARLEY: A hammy Jason Alexander.

GHOST 2: Jane Krakowski, who earlier appeared before Scrooge as a lamplighter he refused to help, arises from the candlelight as the Ghost of Christmas Past.

GHOST 3: Jesse L. Martin (who played a street performer Scrooge had rebuffed) as the Ghost of Christmas Present in full green-robe-and-head-wreath mode. (Also, lots of eye makeup.) Drags Scrooge into a performance that resembles nothing so much as the Radio City Christmas Spectacular.

TINY TIM: Jacob Moriarty as the usual simpering tot.

GHOST 4: Geraldine Chaplin (her first appearance was as a blind beggar who received no charity from Scrooge) as a crone who transforms into a mute, regal ghoul. Yes, even the graveyard has a musical number, which manages to incorporate the funeral-shunning businessmen, Tiny Tim's grave, the junk shop trio, and even a return appearance from Fan and Mother Scrooge into it.

MEMORABLE DIALOGUE: "Tiny Tim, dead? No! His gentle spirit was from God!"

RATING: Despite the fact they were created by composer Alan Menken (*Little Shop of Horrors, Beauty and the Beast*) and lyricist Lynn Ahrens (*Ragtime, Once on This Island*), the songs—and there are *a lot* of them—are pretty awful. This one's quite possibly the worst non-animated adaptation of *A Christmas Carol*.


## THE MODERNIZATIONS

## *An American Christmas Carol* (1979)

**Unrated; 98 min. Written by Jerome Coopersmith. Directed by Eric Till. (Image Entertainment)**

SETTING: New England during the Great Depression

SCROOGE: Benedict Slade (Henry Winkler, buried in thick putty-like makeup), who hands the local orphans cards that say, "You can do it!" and considers that a Christmas present. His S&L Finance Co. forecloses on poor sharecroppers on Christmas Eve, taking away their stoves, rocking chairs, radios, the works. All the people whose items Slade has repossessed will turn up later as the Ghosts.

CRATCHIT: Mr. Thatcher (R. H. Thomson) asks Slade to reopen the local granite quarry for WPA projects and to put the locals back to work. Slade responds by firing him.

MARLEY: Jack Latham (Ken Pogue), "the smartest businessman this state ever knew." No chains; a very cool customer. "Hell's not what you think it is—devil, fire, pitchforks. It's worse."

GHOST 2: Bookseller Merrivale (David Wayne) takes Slade to the orphanage, where kindly furniture manufacturer Mr. Brewster (Chris Wiggins) takes on the troubled young Slade as an apprentice. Brewster's daughter Helen (Susan Hogan) loved Slade. Slade helps put Brewster out of business (as in the 1951 version), and Brewster dies, which adds heft to Susan leaving Slade.

GHOST 3: Orphanage chief Jessup (Gerard Parkes), who appears with all the orphans, singing carols. Gives Slade a glimpse of present-day Helen, now in her own bad old-age makeup, enjoying Christmas with her family, as well as a peek at the Thatchers.

TINY TIM: Jonathan (Chris Cragg)—the only way to cure his polio is to send him to Sister Kenny in Australia, but how can they afford it now that dad has lost his job?

GHOST 4: The Ghost of Christmas Yet to Come appears as Matt Reeves (Dorian Harewood), the sharecropper who is now wearing a wide-open shirt with gold medallions and a black *Saturday Night Fever* suit.

MEMORABLE DIALOGUE: "Never throw good money after bad. And never pay a man one penny more than he's worth."

RATING: Intelligently changes the classic story to fit Depression-era America. If only the makeup were as good as the acting.

# Scrooged (1988)

PG-13; 101 min. Written by Mitch Glazer and Michael O'Donoghue. Directed by Richard Donner. (Paramount Home Video)

SETTING: New York City, the 1980s

SCROOGE: Crass network president Frank Cross (Bill Murray), whose idea of suitable holiday programming is *The Night the Reindeer Died* and *Bob Goulet's Old-Fashioned Cajun Christmas*, not to mention a live version of *Scrooge* (no one ever calls it *A Christmas Carol*) featuring Buddy Hackett, Jamie Farr, the Solid Gold Dancers, and Mary Lou Retton as Tiny Tim. He also fires hapless flunky Eliot Loudermilk (Bobcat Goldthwait) on Christmas Eve.

CRATCHIT: Grace Cooley (Alfre Woodard), Frank's much-put-upon assistant. Frank: "If I work late, you work late. If you can't work late, I can't work late. If I can't work late, *I CAN'T WORK LATE!*"

MARLEY: Lew Hayward (John Forsythe, rotting and dressed in golf-wear), Frank's mentor.

GHOST 2: A decrepit cab driver (David Johansen), whose hack license says "Ghost of Christmas Past."

GHOST 3: A violent pixie (Carol Kane), who smacks Frank around.

TINY TIM: Calvin (Nicholas Phillips), Grace's son, who hasn't spoken since he saw his father killed. (The scene where he solves a puzzle resembles a similar moment in 1986's *The Manhattan Project*.) So when he finally says "God bless us, every one," it's the fact that he talks at all that's so moving.

GHOST 4: First we get a fake one from the *Scrooge*-within-*Scrooged*, but then there's the real one, a terrifying hooded ghost who climbs out of a bank of video monitors to take Frank on an elevator ride to hell.

MEMORABLE DIALOGUE: "The Jews taught me this great word: 'schmuck.' I was a schmuck. And now, I'm not a schmuck!"

RATING: *Scrooged* is kind of overdone and needlessly violent, but Murray's manic final monologue merits sitting through the rest of it.

## *Ebbie* (1995)

**Unrated; 88 min. Written by Paul Redford and Ed Redlich. Directed by George Kaczender. (Not currently available on DVD)**

SETTING: 20th-century USA (as played by Vancouver)

SCROOGE: Elizabeth "Ebbie" Scrooge (Susan Lucci), hard-hearted boss of Dobson's department store.

CRATCHIT: Roberta Cratchet (Wendy Crewson); Ebbie wants her to spend Christmas morning with her family and then come in to work in the afternoon to prepare for the after-Christmas sale.

MARLEY: Jake Marley (Jeffrey DeMunn) died exactly one year ago tonight. "You and me have got to conference." (He's carrying a huge, 1995-ish cell phone.)

GHOST 2: The Dobson's perfume spritzers (Nicole Parker, Jennifer Clement) dressed like bouffant-ed 1960s girl group singers. As they travel through Ebbie's past, their outfits will be updated to astonishingly tacky 1970s and 1980s party-wear.

GHOST 3: Dobson's cranky gift-wrap lady (Lorena Gale) is now the Ghost of Christmas PRESENT, get it?

TINY TIM: Timmy (Taran Noah Smith), who hopes he can skate like the other kids someday. Does a near-falsetto "Angels We Have Heard on High."

GHOST 4: The store's creepy house detective (Bill Croft) as the Spirit of Christmases Yet to Come.

MEMORABLE DIALOGUE: "I sell Christmas, Roberta; I don't buy it."

RATING: There's a real effort to mix things up and make them contemporary. Not the greatest, but it's sweet—and there are several noteworthy performances, including Lucci's.

# Ms. Scrooge (1997)

**Unrated; 88 min. Written by John McGreevey. Directed by John Korty. (Not currently available on DVD)**

SETTING: 20th-century Providence, R.I. (but the buses give it away as Toronto).

SCROOGE: Ebenita Scrooge (Cicely Tyson), the heartless boss of a loan company—first seen putting her foot down on a quarter before a kid can pick it up from the snow. "You'll never get rich that way, kid!" She keeps her coins in several different piggy banks and steam-irons her paper money.

CRATCHIT: John Bourgeois as a nerdy nice guy who owes Ebenita money.

MARLEY: Katherine Helmond as Ebenita's former boss, dead ten years ago Christmas Eve. (Scrooge buried her on Christmas Day so as not to waste a working day.)

GHOST 2: From out of the vault comes the cobweb-covered, white-suited Ghost of Christmas Past (Michael J. Reynolds).

GHOST 3: The somewhat fey Spirit of Christmas Present (Shaun Austin-Olsen).

TINY TIM: A chipper kid (William Greenblatt); Bob puts him on his shoulders and does an ice-slide with him. "Tim has a slow-growing congenital tumor. He's had it since birth. And it's getting worse."

GHOST 4: Spirit of Christmas Yet to Come (Julian Richings), who resembles a funereal Emo Phillips.

MEMORABLE DIALOGUE: "I don't hate Christmas—I *loooove* Christmas! People become overoptimistic, then they overspend, then they overborrow. That's great for my business."

RATING: The acting is terrible; Tyson seems to be impersonating either W. C. Fields or the obscene phone caller in *Black Christmas* (p. 126). A real letdown from the director of *A Christmas Without Snow* (p. 201).

## A Diva's Christmas Carol (2000)

**PG; 120 min. Written and directed by Richard Schenkman. (Paramount Home Video)**

SETTING: Early 21st-century New York City

SCROOGE: Pop singer Ebony Scrooge (Vanessa Williams)—"Just Ebony, if you don't mind."

CRATCHIT: Bob Cratchett (Brian McNamara), who has to tell the band that they have to work on Christmas because Ebony wants to have a concert in NYC on the 25th. (It's allegedly for charity, but it's really just to fill her pockets.)

MARLEY: Marli Jacob (Chilli, from TLC), who died on Christmas Eve in a DUI accident that killed two others. Ebony and Marli had been in a girl group together; after Marli developed a drug problem, Ebony abandoned her, which eventually led to the accident. (Marli's "chains" look like something out of a Janet Jackson video circa *Rhythm Nation*.)

GHOST 2: Kathy Griffin as the Ghost of Christmas Past. She's got a Gucci coat because last year she had to show Tom Ford his past Christmases.

GHOST 3: Hard-partying rocker Ghost of Christmas Present (John Taylor of Duran Duran)—or Steve, if you prefer—with a trio of groupies.

TINY TIM: Little Tim (Joshua Archambault), Bob's son—he's got anemia and high blood pressure but the doctors can't seem to figure out what's wrong with him.

GHOST 4: A no-holds-barred *VH1's Behind the Music* of Ebony. ("Charges of cruelty and miserliness were made, but never stuck." "The remarkable life—and tragic death—of a diva.") It features the voice of Jim Forbes, the actual *Behind the Music* narrator, and interviews with real-life musicians Nile Rodgers and Brian McKnight as well as other characters from the story.

MEMORABLE DIALOGUE: Ebony: "Do I have to start yelling?" (after she's already been doing that for some time)

RATING: A funny take on the material with a savvy pop-culture spin. Who knew the only thing scarier than a hooded wraith is an unflattering cable documentary?

## *A Carol Christmas* (2003)

**Unrated; 88 min. Written by Tom Amundsen. Directed by Matthew Irmas. (Good Times Home Video)**

SETTING: Early 21st-century Los Angeles, where there's not a single snowflake to be found.

SCROOGE: Self-centered child star–turned–talk show host Carol Cartman (Tori Spelling).

CRATCHIT: Her overworked assistant Roberta Timmons (Nina Siemaszko).

MARLEY: Carol's Aunt Marla (Dinah Manoff), her agent and the talk show's original producer, who taught Carol how to be ruthless and cruel. When Carol takes a pre-show nap, Marla appears, bedecked in gold chains, telling her, "Be nice!"

GHOST 2: None other than Gary Coleman pops up as the Ghost of Christmas Past.

GHOST 3: The Ghost of Christmas Present takes the form of a rival chat show host, the platitude-spouting Dr. Bob (William Shatner).

TINY TIM: Lily (Holliston Coleman), whom Carol refers to as "Tiny Timmons." She's not sickly-sweet like the usual Tiny Tims; putting her in the middle of a custody case (her newly remarried deadbeat dad wants to take her away from Roberta), instead of making us feel sorry for her infirmity, makes the character less of a tear-jerking conceit.

GHOST 4: A pale, grim-faced limo driver with a stretch Hummer. He takes Carol to a future Christmas where her show has become even more tacky and exploitive; she walks off the set. Then he shows her an older Carol, grey-haired, frumpy and driving a crappy old car to a retirement-home opening. (After she cuts the ribbon, she has to stand on the corner with one of those arrow signs.)

MEMORABLE DIALOGUE: Carol: "You're that guy who used to have a TV show!" Ghost of Christmas Past: "There's not much work for a middle-aged actor who's even too small to be a jockey."

RATING: Fluffy, but more fun than you'd think.


## THE ANIMATED VERSIONS

## *Mickey's Christmas Carol* (1983)

G; 26 min. Written by Burny Mattinson, Tony Marino, Ed Gombert, Don Griffith, Alan Young, and Alan Dinehart. Directed by Burny Mattinson. (Walt Disney Home Entertainment)

SETTING: A Victorian England lousy with anthropomorphized animals. Even within species they look different—Mickey Mouse is Bob Cratchit while the Basil of Baker Street (from 1986's *The*

*Great Mouse Detective*), who looks more like an actual mouse, is there to raise funds for the poor.

SCROOGE: Scrooge McDuck (voiced by Alan Young), in the role he was born to play. (Donald, voiced by Clarence Nash, plays nephew Fred. The fact that Fred, a duck, plans to serve roast goose with chestnut dressing on Christmas is never addressed.)

MARLEY: Goofy (Hal Smith), who's got the Marley accessories but still speaks with his own "Gawrsh!"-type exclamations.

GHOST 2: Jiminy Cricket (Eddie Carroll) as the Ghost of Christmas Past. (He sports a button that says "Ghost of Christmas Past—Official.") "Fezzywig" is Mr. Toad; most of the party guests are characters from various Disney features. Daisy Duck is Isabel.

GHOST 3: Willie the Giant (Will Ryan) from *Mickey and the Beanstalk* (1947).

TINY TIM: Voiced by Dick Billingsley, he's kind of a . . . mini-Mickey.

GHOST 4: Cigar-chomping Black Pete (also Ryan). British-accented weasels dig Scrooge's grave, and there's a vision of hellfire through his casket.

MEMORABLE DIALOGUE: Scrooge: "My partner, Jacob Marley, dead seven years today. Ah, he was a good'un: he robbed from the widows and swindled the poor. In his will, he left me enough money to pay for his tombstone—and I had him buried at sea!"

RATING: At just 26 minutes, it zips through the Dickens tale quickly enough for the youngest audiences. The one new song written for it will escape your brain as quickly as it enters.

## *A Christmas Carol* (1997)

**PG (some scary images); 72 min. Written by Jymn Magon. Directed by Stan Phillips. (Warner Home Video)**

SETTING: A poorly animated Victorian London

SCROOGE: A miser (the voice of Tim Curry, not sounding a whole lot like Tim Curry) with a grumpy bulldog named Debit.

CRATCHIT: Michael York.

MARLEY: Headwrap and chains, but a 20th-century businessman's suit. Voiced by Ed Asner, sort of attempting a British accent.

GHOST 1: A mischievous young boy Ghost of Christmas Past takes Scrooge *and* the dog to the schoolroom, where young Scrooge sings about how he reads books in an attempt not to be sad. Later, Belle (Jodi Benson) dumps him in song.

GHOST 2: A woman (Whoopi Goldberg, affecting a ridiculous accent) sporting the green robe and holly in her hair. The Cratchits sing a song, expressing differing views on Scrooge, called "Random Acts of Kindness," and Fred performs the silly "Santa's Sooty Suit."

TINY TIM: Jarrad Kritzstein. He, like young Scrooge, enjoys reading in front of the fire.

GHOST 3: No face, cloaked ghost.

MEMORABLE DIALOGUE: Scrooge, as the second ghost takes him flying: "I've got to get a lock for that window."

RATING: Terribly animated, generally forgettable. Even for kids, there are better versions.

## *An All Dogs Christmas Carol* (1998)

G; 73 min. Written by Jymn Magon. Directed by Paul Sabella and Gary Selvaggio. (MGM Home Video)

SETTING: The Flea Bite Café in San Francisco, and all the characters are dogs.

SCROOGE: Carface (Ernest Borgnine), a cruel canine loan shark with a dog whistle that hypnotizes his fellow mutts into handing over all their bones; he also steals their food, their toys, and the money raised for Timmy's (see below) operation for good measure.

Carface works for a dog-witch named Belladonna (Bebe Neu-wirth), who has a plot to ruin Christmas.

CRATCHIT: Killer (Charles Nelson Reilly), a nerdy accountant/ sycophant.

MARLEY: Charlie (Steven Weber)—disguised as "Jacob Charlie"— magically hosts a TV special called *It's a Wonderful Carface* and warns Carface of the impending appearance of the three ghosts.

GHOST 2: Itchy (Dom DeLuise) as the Ghost of Christmas Past. We learn that Carface's young owner was mean to the dog, which made him become a hoodlum.

GHOST 3: Sasha (Sheena Easton), with a wreath of candles on her head.

TINY TIM: Timmy (Taylor Emerson), a puppy with a lame leg— he's got a human owner, but the dogs have to raise money for his operation?

GHOST 4: A faceless spectre who turns out to be Charlie in a yellow zoot suit.

MEMORABLE DIALOGUE: "We're going to run a scam on Carface. A *Dickens* of a scam!"

RATING: Really young kids may find this charming. (It's a tiny bit better than the awful 1997 animated version from the same screenwriter.) Adults might enjoy Reilly's typically over-the-top performance. The songs are pretty dreadful, though.

## Christmas Carol: The Movie (2001)

**PG; 77 min. Written by Piet Kroon and Robert Llewellyn. Directed by Jimmy T. Murakami. (MGM Home Video)**

SETTING: A Victorian London full of odd-looking people with jerky movements.

SCROOGE: Simon Callow, who also provides the voice of a narrating Charles Dickens.

CRATCHIT: Rhys Ifans, stripped clean of almost any personality.

MARLEY: A miscast Nicolas Cage. "Grow! Blossom! Share, Ebenezer! Mend your ways!"

GHOST 2: Flame-haired girl (Jane Horrocks) whose face suddenly grows old.

GHOST 3: Big brown beard, big brown robe. Michael Gambon has a perfect voice for Christmas Past.

TINY TIM: Sickly Tim is taken out of bed to join the family at dinner. His pneumonia returned because Scrooge dumped a bucket of freezing water on him.

GHOST 4: Scrooge gets carried off by Marley and the other unhappy spirits.

RATING: Despite the presence of many talented actors, this cheaply animated entry ranks among the worst of the *Christmas Carol* adaptations. Somehow, the film's theme song "What If"—sung by Kate Winslet, not previously known for her musical prowess—made it to Number Six on the UK singles charts.

## *Barbie in A Christmas Carol* (2008)

**Unrated; 60 min. Written by Elise Allen. Directed by William Lau. (Universal Studios Home Entertainment)**

SETTING: Barbie's dream house, where younger sister Kelly (voiced by Amelia Henderson) is being bratty about going to the charity ball; she'd rather stay home and drink cocoa and sing carols and do the usual family traditions. So Barbie (Kelly Sheridan) tells her a story about . . .

SCROOGE: Eden Starling (Morwenna Banks), "the most famous singing star in Victorian England." She has a cat named Chuzzlewit (for you Dickens fans) and is a total pain-in-the-rump diva.

MARLEY: Her Aunt Marie (Pam Hyatt), the theatre's original owner, who raised Eden and told her that, "In a selfish world, the selfish succeed." Rather than lockboxes, her ghostly chains are all attached to mirrors.

GHOST 2: A little girl (Tabitha St. Germain) with a ponytail shows young Eden in a grim house with no Christmas décor whatsoever. Aunt Marie insists she rehearse rather than go visit friends for the holiday.

GHOST 3: A plump, red-haired woman (Kathleen Barr) in a green gown.

TINY TIM: Tammy (Henderson), a hobbling orphan who looks just like Kelly. Eden isn't touched as much by Tammy's plight as by the prospect of the orphanage closing down.

GHOST 4: A pretty lady (Gwynyth Walsh) wearing a hooded cape. (No faceless spectres or skeletal figures here.) "The future isn't like the past; every choice you make alters the rest."

MEMORABLE DIALOGUE: "Excuse me, my job is Gad's Hill Theatre costume designer, not crumpet-butterizer."

RATING: Heinous computer animation—the eerie human faces are nearly as disturbing as the ones in the 2009 version—but it's possibly the least scary Christmas Carol adaptation ever, perfect for little girls who might have a problem with ghosts.

## A Christmas Carol (2009)

PG (scary sequences and images); 98 min. Written and directed by Robert Zemeckis. (Walt Disney Home Entertainment)

SETTING: Victorian London, meticulously detailed and packed with people with rubbery faces and dead eyes.

SCROOGE: A cruel, mop-headed moneylender voiced by Jim Carrey.

CRATCHIT: He speaks with Gary Oldman's voice and resembles a bobblehead version of the actor.

MARLEY: Oldman again, bearing the character's traditional chains.

GHOST 2: Carrey again, as a burning candle with a face of fire. (Bob Hoskins' Fezziwig seems to look the least freakish of this lot after being converted to a motion-capture animated character.)

GHOST 3: Once more, Carrey, in the traditional green robe and red beard, and with an accent that wobbles between Scottish and Liverpudlian. A direct quote from Dickens—Scrooge blames the Ghost of Christmas Present for a law that closed bakeries on Sunday—zips by so fast that it will make no sense to anyone who hasn't recently read the annotated version of the original story footnoted by Dickens scholar Michael Patrick Hearn.

TINY TIM: Motion-capture Gary Oldman. As a child. It's as skin-crawling as it sounds.

GHOST 4: A faceless spectre who shrinks Scrooge down to tiny size so he can run through the gutters. Because this story really needed some chase scenes.

MEMORABLE DIALOGUE: "Tuppence is tuppence," says Scrooge, as he removes the pennies from dead Marley's eyes.

RATINGS: At times, this adaptation is so faithful to the original as to be bewildering; at others, it becomes an action movie designed to show off the 3-D technology. In any event, the motion-capture animation of human beings is still creepy-looking at this stage of the game, making this as difficult to stomach as Zemeckis' other unintentionally unsettling Christmas extravaganza, *The Polar Express* (2004). (You'd never guess that *Avatar*, featuring far better mo-cap work, opened in theaters just a month or so later.)

## THE LOOSEST AND LEAST-KNOWN ADAPTATION, WHICH NONETHELESS DESPERATELY NEEDS TO BE RELEASED ON DVD

### *Carol for Another Christmas* (1964)

Unrated; 84 min. Written by Rod Serling. Directed by Joseph L. Mankiewicz. (Not currently available on DVD)

SETTING: USA, Christmas Eve 1964

SCROOGE: Daniel Grudge (Sterling Hayden), a rich and powerful man who, embittered over the wartime death of his son Marley (Peter Fonda), advocates for isolationism and suspicion of other nations. His nephew Fred (Ben Gazzara) also loved Marley, and he tells Grudge that there's no room for fences in the modern world.

GHOST 1: Grudge sees an apparition of Marley, a record starts playing "Don't Sit Under the Apple Tree," and suddenly Grudge is on a World War I troop transport with the Ghost of Christmas Past (Steve Lawrence). They're surrounded by the caskets of soldiers, draped in flags of many nations. Grudge says the U.S. shouldn't have been involved in WWI, and that anyone who died to make the world safe for democracy is a sucker. The Ghost replies that it's important that nations talk to each other, because when they're talking, they're not fighting. He also points out that post-war isolationism is what allowed Hitler to take so much of Europe.

GHOST 2: Grudge finds himself back in Hiroshima, after the atomic bomb was dropped, where he had served during the war. A WAVE (Eva Marie Saint) is horrified to see bombing victims who no longer have faces. Grudge says the arithmetic of dropping the bomb saved lives on both sides. She points out that they're standing in the middle of what used to be a city—where almost as many people died in one day as the Confederates lost in the entire Civil War—and that war itself might soon be obsolete since we could destroy the whole planet in a few afternoons. She asks him not to call the death and maiming of thousands "arithmetic" anymore.

GHOST 3: The Ghost of Christmas Present (Pat Hingle) sits at the head of a well-stocked table and makes a glutton of himself, when he's just yards away from a refugee camp filled with displaced, hungry people. Grudge asks how he can ignore the suffering people right next to him, and the Ghost asks Grudge how many times he's stuffed himself, knowing that two-thirds of the world is starving. The Ghost throws back Grudge's earlier comments about how the needy should fend for themselves and how the government should spend their money on more bombers.

GHOST 4: Grudge enters a bombed-out town hall and meets the Ghost of Christmas Future (Robert Shaw). There are no calendars, no electricity, and very few people left after the war in the future. Grudge asks about the United Nations; the Ghost tells him they dropped out and the conversation stopped. A motley band of survivors appear, led by "the non-imperial ME" (Peter Sellers). ME tells his followers that they have to look out for themselves, and that those other tribes who want to negotiate with them really want to take them over, and that they must be destroyed. Charles (Percy Rodrigues), Grudge's butler, tries to get ME to listen to reason; a young boy shoots him. When Grudge awakes, he realizes that he needs to rethink his views on internationalism and humanity.

MEMORABLE DIALOGUE: "I'm in no mood for the brotherhood of man."

RATING: While occasionally heavy-handed (in the way that Rod Serling could sometimes be when trying to make a political point), *Carol for Another Christmas* is so uniquely powerful and well acted (the extraordinary cast also includes James Shigeta and Britt Ekland) that this fascinatingly odd little film needs to be made more readily available. Produced by the United Nations, the TV special aired once, on December 28, 1964; it can be viewed at the Paley Centers for Media in Los Angeles and New York City.

# THE SCROOGIE AWARDS, RECOGNIZING THE VIRTUES AND VICES OF THE MANY MOVIES MADE FROM *A CHRISTMAS CAROL*

BEST SCROOGE: Alastair Sim, *A Christmas Carol* (1951), with Albert Finney and George C. Scott as close runners-up.

BEST MARLEY: Statler and Waldorf as the Marley Brothers, *A Muppet Christmas Carol*.

BEST GHOST OF CHRISTMAS PAST: Dame Edith Evans, doing an ethereal spin on her Aunt Augusta from *The Importance of Being Earnest* (1952), in *Scrooge* (1970).

BEST GHOST OF CHRISTMAS PRESENT: Edward Woodward, who brusquely shoots down any and all of Scrooge's gripes, in *A Christmas Carol* (1984).

BEST GHOST OF CHRISTMAS YET TO COME: The brutally frank *Behind the Music* episode in *A Diva's Christmas Carol*.

BEST TINY TIM (MALE): The exuberant Gerald McBoingBoing in *Mister Magoo's Christmas Carol*.

BEST TINY TIM (FEMALE): Lily (Holliston Coleman) in *A Carol Christmas*.

MOST WET-EYED TINY TIM: As great as *Scrooge* (1970) is, Richard Beaumont all but cries "Love me!" in his turn as one of Dickens' most shamefully sentimental characters.

BEST ANIMATED VERSION: *Mister Magoo's Christmas Carol*

WORST ANIMATED VERSION: In a very competitive category, dishonors go to the 1997 *A Christmas Carol*, where Scrooge's bulldog accompanies him on his Christmas Eve journeys. But *An All Dogs Christmas Carol* and *Christmas Carol: The Movie* are close runners-up.

MOST FAITHFUL ADAPTATION: For including such often-overlooked details as the coal miners and the lighthouse keepers, the indebted couple, and Ignorance and Want, the 1999 *A Christmas Carol* starring Patrick Stewart sticks closest to Dickens' original story.

BEST OF THE "SCROOGE IS A RUTHLESSLY AMBITIOUS WOMAN" TV MOVIES: *A Diva's Christmas Carol*.

WORST OF THE "SCROOGE IS A RUTHLESSLY AMBITIOUS WOMAN" TV MOVIES: *Ms. Scrooge*.

MOST WRITERS PER MINUTE: *Mickey's Christmas Carol*, which runs a mere 26 minutes but still required the services of six people adapting Charles Dickens.

HARDEST-WORKING MEN IN SCROOGE BUSINESS: Frank Oz and Steve Whitmire, who voiced seven characters a piece in *The Muppet Christmas Carol*.

# CHAPTER 8

José Luis "Trotsky" Aguirre and José Elias Moreno in *Santa Claus* (1959).

# The Worst Christmas (Movies) Ever
## LUMPS OF COAL IN YOUR CINEMA STOCKING

In the same way that a small child's ineptly constructed ornament—shedding glitter, covered in glue, bearing misspelled words—can become a cherished item that you look forward to putting on your tree every year, some movies similarly become adorable disasters, enjoyable for their wonderful awfulness. These films are so unbelievably misguided that you have to pop them in every Christmas to remind yourself that you didn't dream the whole thing after too many sugarplums.

There's no shortage of terrible Christmas movies—plenty of them are listed in the Appendix (p. 219)—but only a few are so wonderfully wretched that they wind up being thoroughly entertaining, although not in ways that the filmmakers intended. Some of the following films took themselves way too seriously, while others were clearly made by people who figured that children would sit through *any* flickering images for an hour or so, no matter how inept and moronic. Either way, the movies in this chapter are cinematic gifts so terrible that you won't be able to bring yourself to return them. (Several titles aren't available on DVD, but it's worth your while to seek them out on cable or on old VHS tapes. Seriously.)

## *The Christmas That Almost Wasn't (Il Natale che quasi non fu)* (1966)

G; 89 min. Screenplay by Paul Tripp, based on his book. Directed by Rossano Brazzi. Starring Rossano Brazzi, Paul Tripp, Mischa Auer, Alberto Rabagliati. (Hen's Tooth Video)

On the eve of his annual trip around the world to give out presents, Santa Claus (Rabagliati) gets the bad news that mean old millionaire Phineas T. Prune (Brazzi) has bought the North Pole and plans to foreclose on Santa's workshop in order to cancel Christmas. (This is one of those stories where the message is: No presents, no Christmas. Did we learn nothing from the Grinch's assault on Whoville?) Santa asks kindly attorney Mr. Whipple (Tripp) for help; Whipple's big idea is to get his client a job as a department store Santa so he can raise the money to pay back Prune—only to have Prune buy the store and force Santa and Whipple to hand over their salaries to pay for toys they broke. When all seems lost, the children of the world are there to give Santa a hand—but can St. Nick teach Prune to love Christmas?

It's interesting to watch, through modern eyes, what used to be considered suitable entertainment for kids: When Santa says, "I've lost count of all the children I've seen asleep in their beds," or sings "I've Got a Date with Children," you'll have to remind yourself not to dial 9-1-1. But hindsight aside, *The Christmas That Almost Wasn't* is a dismal affair, featuring tuneless and forgettable songs, downright ugly production design, choppy dubbing, and some very odd-looking elves wearing ladies' wigs; the latter group includes veteran character actor Mischa Auer (whose credits include the classic 1936 screwball comedy *My Man Godfrey* and Orson Welles' 1955 *Mr. Arkadin*). If this bizarre kiddie flick didn't scar you as a child, give it an opportunity to do so as an adult.

**FUN FACTS**

- Actor Brazzi (perhaps most famous for playing the plantation owner in *South Pacific* [1958] who duets with Mitzi Gaynor on "Some Enchanted Evening") made his directorial debut here. Tripp had created *Mr. I. Magination,* one of the very first children's television shows, and Rabagliati was once known as "the Bing Crosby of Italy."

- *Variety* noted "it will take some doting parents to sit through [the] entire film," while *The New York Times* called it "a fairly pleasant but highly derivative fable, with some animation and a half-dozen songs that might entrance the younger pre-teens but is likely to bore almost everyone else." The *New York World Journal Tribune* pointed out the film's "leaden archness"—and pronounced Tripp's songs "hopeless," while the *New York Post* lamented, "Mischa Auer, poor fellow, is in for a minor role that lets him make a few faces. Who wouldn't make faces if he had to go through much of this?"

- Brazzi became involved with the film after the script was offered to his wife, Lydia Brazzi, who was cast as Mrs. Claus. The producer asked him to direct and to play the villain, and the actor acquiesced. Or so the publicity notes say, anyway.

## *Get Yourself a College Girl* (1964)

Unrated; 87 min. Written by Robert E. Kent. Directed by Sidney Miller. Starring Mary Ann Mobley, Nancy Sinatra, the Animals, the Dave Clark Five. (Not currently available on DVD)

Terry (Mobley) attends a conservative college for women, but on the side she's the popular writer of provocative hit pop songs. Her overzealous music publisher Gary (Chad Everett) makes Terry's double life public, resulting in her suspension from school. Meanwhile,

Terry travels to Sun Valley for a Christmas ski trip with her best friend Lynne (Sinatra)—who's secretly married and rendezvousing with her husband—and dance professor Marge ( Joan O'Brien), and they all get involved in a benefit concert for a senator (Willard Waterman) seeking re-election.

Even by Frankie-and-Annette beach party movie standards—replace the sand with snow, and that's pretty much what we're dealing with here—*Get Yourself a College Girl* is ridiculously bubble-headed. MGM may have been able to provide better production values than some of the B-movie studios turning out similar films (Hair Styles by Sydney Guilaroff!), but all the gloss in the world doesn't make the script any less inane. It's still a fun sit, though, for reasons good and bad—the bad is the utter inanity of the plot and the wide-eyed blankness of Sinatra and Mobley (the 1959 Miss America makes her movie debut here, and it shows); what the movie has going for it is an impressive array of pop acts of the era. Besides the Dave Clark Five and the Animals, *College Girl* offers the only big-screen appearance of legendary Brazilian vocalist Astrud Gilberto, singing "The Girl from Ipanema" with the Stan Getz Quartet backing her up. Turn this one on at Christmastime to enjoy the musical performances, but don't deprive yourself of the blistering stupidity going on between songs.

**FUN FACTS**

- *College Girl* producer Sam Katzman was a legend in exploitation filmmaking going all the way back to the early days of talking pictures; his extensive credits include serials (like 1946's *Hop Harrigan*), Westerns, jungle adventures, monster movies, and Elvis vehicles. His production slate for 1956 alone included *Inside Detroit, Perils of the Wilderness, The Houston Story, Uranium Boom, Rock Around the Clock, Blackjack Ketchum, Desperado, The Werewolf, Earth vs. the Flying Saucers, Blazing the Overland Trail, Miami Expose, Cha-Cha-Cha Boom!, Don't Knock the Rock,* and *Rumble on the Docks.*

- Nancy Sinatra does not sing in the movie, but two years later she'd hit the pop charts with "These Boots Were Made for Walkin'." The producers of *Get Yourself a College Girl* clearly knew the guest musicians—who dominate the posters—and not the stars were the film's main draw. (Tag line: "The swingin'-est blast ever filmed!")
- Mobley was the first woman to be voted into the University of Mississippi Hall of Fame, alongside such notables as William Faulkner. One wonders if the selection committee ever saw *Get Yourself a College Girl*.

## *The Magic Christmas Tree* (1964)

**Unrated; 60 min. Written by Harold Vaughn Taylor. Directed by Richard C. Parish. Starring Chris Kroesen, Valerie Hobbs, Robert Maffei, Darlene Lohnes. (Not currently available on DVD)**

OK, so these kids have a long conversation about Halloween at school, and later that day, one of them helps the neighborhood's weird old lady get her cat Lucifer out of a tree. The kid bumps his head and suddenly the movie's in color and the old lady says she's a witch. To thank him, she gives him a ring with a magical seed inside—if he plants the seed under the wishbone of a Thanksgiving turkey, he'll get a Christmas tree that will grant three wishes. So then there's this talking tree that the kid's dad can't chop down, and then the kid's parents and sister choose the evening of Christmas Eve to go out shopping. The kid asks the tree for "an hour of absolute power," which apparently gives him the ability to redecorate and to play stupid pranks that involve firemen and pie fights. Then he asks to have Santa all to himself, so the tree kidnaps the jolly old man, but then the kid meets a giant in the forest and realizes he's been selfish so he uses his third wish to cancel the second wish. And then he wakes up. THE END.

It's hard to do justice to the flat-out looniness of this low-budget movie, but the story features such an odd mix of the occult, bad slapstick comedy, and elementary-school surrealism that one won-ders if this nutty tale wasn't really churned out by an 11-year-old writer hopped up on Bosco. The tree has one of those fey and bitchy voices of the Paul Lynde–Charles Nelson Reilly school, and don't be surprised if the old witch lady reminds you of Little Edie Beale from *Grey Gardens* (1975). Still, *The Magic Christmas Tree* exerts that strange fascination that only the best bad movies can muster—you'll sit there, agog at the thought that anyone felt this was a good idea or that its makers watched the footage with confidence that entertain-ment was being created.

**FUN FACTS**

- Many of the film's crew—including director Parish, executive producer Fred C. Gerrior, and composer Victor Kirk—have no other movie credits. Among the cast, one of the few to work else-where was Robert "Big Buck" Maffei, who plays the giant; he went on to play Brobdingnagian characters on TV's *Lost in Space* and *Star Trek*.

- The poster for the film's theatrical release promised "Holiday Ad-venture that dazzles your eyes . . . fills you with fun! SEE! The Magic Ring! Fantastic! Unbelievable! SEE! The Crazy Police Car and Fire Engine Chase! SEE! The Evil Witch and More!" (Be-cause of *Magic Christmas Tree*'s abbreviated running time, it was often paired in theatrical engagements with the 1948 Max Fleisch-er short *Rudolph the Red-Nosed Reindeer*.)

## *Santa and the Ice Cream Bunny* (1972)

G; 96 min. No writer credited. Directed by Barry Mahon and R. Winer. Starring Jay Ripley, Kim Nicholas, Shay Garner. (Not currently avail-able on DVD)

Santa's elves sing an incoherent song (Sample lyrics: "Tra-la-la-la-la-la But where is Santa Claus?/Tra-la-la-la-la-la Santa isn't here") and manhandle store-bought toys. Meanwhile, Santa Claus (Ripley) finds himself stuck on a Florida beach, abandoned by his flying reindeer who couldn't take the heat of the Sunshine State. Santa rallies the local children—including one who's jumping off the roof of his house holding a giant patio umbrella; don't try this at home, kids!—to come help him out. (Tom Sawyer and Huck Finn drift in on a raft as well. Don't ask.) The kids try attaching various animals (a cow, a pig, a sheep, a guy in a gorilla costume, etc.) to the sleigh, but none of the beasts can budge the thing. Santa tells the kids they've got to believe in their dreams and never give up, which prompts him to launch into the story of Thumbelina, which is clearly a whole other movie—a featurette filmed at no-longer-extant Florida theme park Pirate's World—that's been stuck inside this one. Once the cheesy fable has ended, the kids figure out a solution—they go to Pirate's World and fetch the Ice Cream Bunny, who rides an old-timey fire truck to the beach. He picks up Santa in the truck and takes him home.

There's maybe five minutes of actual story here, but director Winer (Mahon did the "Thumbelina" section) pads out every individual moment past its breaking point. Santa sings a lament about being stuck on the beach, and the sequence goes on and on. The kids come running to help him, and the sequence goes on and on. The kids run to fetch animals, and . . . you get the picture. No line ("You'll help me, won't you, kids?") is uttered once when it can be repeated five times. Then there's the "Thumbelina" segment, about a teen girl who goes to the theater at Pirate's World and checks out a terrible stage version of the Hans Christian Andersen fable, and that eats up a good (or bad) 45 minutes or so. One can imagine the scarring effects this movie must have had on the poor kids who actually suffered through it in the theater—Santa looks drunk and overheated, and the Ice Cream Bunny (whose name is never explained) sports an animal costume which, according to website The Agony Booth, resembles "a ratty, torn-up bunny suit that the filmmakers probably found in a dumpster behind a shopping mall." If ever a movie begged for an eggnog drinking game, *Santa and the Ice Cream Bunny* is it; the Zapruder footage represents more sophisticated filmmaking.

**FUN FACTS**

- Barry Mahon's previous directorial efforts included such family-friendly films as *The Diary of Knockers McCalla* (1968), *Fanny Hill Meets Dr. Erotico* (1967), and *The Adventures of Busty Brown* (1964). He's probably best known for directing the Red Scare thriller *Rocket Attack USA* (1961)—which later earned a fervent mocking on the cable series *Mystery Science Theater 3000*—as well as Errol Flynn's last movie, *Cuban Rebel Girls* (1959).
- Kim Nicholas—who played one of the Florida kids as well as one of Santa's elves—was the only juvenile cast member who went on to have any kind of film career, playing opposite William Shatner in the disturbing also-shot-in-Florida thriller *Impulse* (1974) and as "Girl Hostage" in John Frankenheimer's *Black Sunday* (1977).
- Pirate's World, which closed in 1975 after Walt Disney World opened, figures into another awful Christmas movie: Some versions of the dreadful animated film *Santa and the Three Bears* (1970) feature insert shots of wild animals at the park filmed by none other than Barry Mahon.

## *Santa Claus* (1959)

Unrated; 94 min. Written by Adolfo Torres Portillo and René Cardona. Directed by René Cardona. Starring José Elías Moreno, José Luis "Trotsky" Aguirre, Lupita Quezadas, Armando Arriola. (Westlake Entertainment Group)

As Christmas Day approaches, Santa Claus (Moreno) prepares to brings toys to all the good children of the world with the assistance of his staff of magical helpers. Satan hopes to destroy Santa Claus and sends the demon Pitch (Aguirre) to Earth to create havoc on Christmas Eve. Pitch focuses on three mean little boys, encouraging them to make mischief, and he also tries to convince poor young Lupita (Quezadas) to steal a doll rather than to believe that Santa will bring her one. Santa makes a little rich boy's wishes come true by sending the child's parents home to spend more time with him—it involves a "cocktail of remembrance," long story—but Pitch sabotages Santa's magic sleep powder and the flower that allows him to become invisible. Can Merlin (Arriola) save the day before the sun rises on December 25?

*¡Ay, ay, ay!* Leave it to the director of *Wrestling Women vs. the Aztec Mummy* (1964) to come up with a children's entertainment this mind-bogglingly bizarre. Santa and Merlin teaming up to battle the devil is just one of *Santa Claus'* truly weird qualities—Lupita's nightmare about giant dancing dolls is the kind of movie moment that sent a generation of children into therapy—making for one wacky holiday film. Kids who grew up in the southwest in the 1960s and '70s were subjected to this low-budget production at annual kiddie matinees every December, but *Santa Claus* became a more widely known cult favorite after it got the skewering it so richly deserved on *Mystery Science Theater 3000*. After your first exposure to *Santa Claus*, watch out: Its crazy energetic pull will have you going back for just one more look (because the last time you couldn't quite believe your own eyes) every Christmas if you're not careful. Each viewing reveals fresh Santa-insanity.

**FUN FACTS**
- *Santa Claus* was released in the United States by K. Gordon Murray, the infamous "King of the Kiddie Matinee," who would cheaply acquire rights to European and Mexican fairy-tale movies, dub them into English, and repackage them for American audiences. Murray also narrates the English-language version of *Santa Claus* under the name "Ken Smith."

- Somehow, *Santa Claus* won the Golden Gate Award for the Best Family Film at the 1959 San Francisco International Film Festival.
- In a way, *Santa Claus* is, in many Spanish-speaking countries, the equivalent of *It's a Wonderful Life*—when the film's copyright lapsed and went into the public domain, TV stations aired it over and over again at Christmastime, thus making it a cherished holiday tradition in many nations.
- After the film was shown on *Mystery Science Theater 3000*, "Pitch" (as played by Paul Chaplin) became a recurring character on the show.

## Santa Claus Conquers the Martians (1964)

**Unrated; 86 min. Written by Glenville Mareth; story by Paul L. Jacobson. Directed by Nicholas Webster. Starring John Call, Bill McCutcheon, Leonard Hicks, Pia Zadora. (Alpha Video and other sources)**

The children of Mars, who are treated like adults and have never been allowed to laugh and play, spend their days glumly glued to TV broadcasts from Earth, particularly those shows dealing with Santa Claus (Call). Concerned about the young people, Martian ruler Kimar (Hicks) organizes an expedition to kidnap Santa and to bring him to the red planet. Clumsy Dropo (McCutcheon) tags along, and the Martians also wind up kidnapping Earth kids Billy (Victor Stiles) and Betty (Donna Conforti) for their valuable Santa-related intel. Back on Mars, the evil Voldar (Vincent Beck) tries to eliminate Santa, but he accidentally makes off with Dropo, dressed in the red suit, instead. Santa eventually realizes that Dropo can become the new Martian Santa, so the jolly old man bids farewell to the kids of Mars—including Kimar's daughter, Girmar (Zadora, in her screen debut)—and returns to Earth with Billy and Betty.

When people talk about bad movies, you hear terms like "cardboard sets," "amateurish acting" and "ridiculous concept" thrown

around willy-nilly, but few celluloid stinkers reach the depths of
*Santa Claus Conquers the Martians*, a movie that combines a loony
high-concept plot (it's all there in the title), condescending filmmaking (there should be a genre called "Make It Really Stupid—It's
for Kids"), and a thoroughly pervasive sense of inanity. It's a film
that's best enjoyed in the mocking versions prepared by *Mystery
Science Theater 3000* or Cinematic Titanic (both are available on
DVD), but even on its own, *Martians* plays well to a roomful of sarcastic viewers who will nonetheless find themselves dumbfounded.
The film has its defenders—David J. Hogan, in *Filmfax* magazine,
suggested that *Martians* is a metaphor for the soullessness of industrial society, "a kind of *Metropolis* [1927] for nine-year-olds"—but
most aficionados of cinematic disasters put this stinker on their
naughty list.

**FUN FACTS**
- The film was shot in just ten days for a budget of less than
  $200,000. And it shows.
- McCutcheon's brand of broad slapstick must play better onstage
  than in the movies—he won a Tony for the 1987 revival of *Anything Goes*. (Generations of kids also know him as Uncle Wally, a
  role he played on *Sesame Street* between 1984 and 1992.)
- *Boxoffice* magazine noted, "[T]he picture will have strong appeal
  to the tots and the younger teenagers although a lobby sign with
  'No One Admitted OVER 16 Years of Age' might be appropriate,
  for most adult patrons are likely to find it overly saccharine and
  nonsensical. With no marquee names, the title is the only selling
  point."
- *Santa Claus Conquers the Martians* has been adapted into several
  tongue-in-cheek stage musicals; the first was a 1993 Chicago production adapted and directed by Sean Abley, followed by a 2006
  version created by Brian Newell in Fullerton, Calif. The punk
  band Sloppy Seconds covered the film's irritating-but-catchy

theme song "Hooray for Santa Claus" for the 1995 compilation *Punk Rock Christmas*.

## *Santa Claus: The Movie* (1985)

PG; 107 min. Written by David Newman; story by David Newman and Leslie Newman. Directed by Jeannot Szwarc. Starring David Huddleston, Dudley Moore, John Lithgow, Burgess Meredith. (Anchor Bay Entertainment)

The story begins in the 14th century, when woodcutter Claus (Huddleston) and his wife Anya (Judy Cornwell) brave terrible winter storms to bring his toys to all the boys and girls of the area on Christmas Eve. The couple, and their reindeer Donner and Blitzen, get trapped in a blizzard, but they are rescued and transported away to the top of the world by tiny people known as the Vendequm. The Vendequm, who prefer to be known as "elves," have been waiting for Claus—they make toys, and now they have someone who will deliver them to children all over the world. One of the elves, Patch (Moore), has ideas for modernizing the process. Some of his notions are good ones—giving Santa a red suit instead of a green one, for instance—but his mechanization of the factory leads to second-rate toys that immediately break. Patch runs away in shame, traveling to modern-day New York City, where he goes to work for evil toy manufacturer BZ (Lithgow). Can Santa bring Patch home where he belongs before BZ destroys Christmas?

Father-and-son producers Alexander and Ilya Salkind apparently hoped to recapture the magic of their hit film *Superman* (1978) by exploring the origin of another iconic hero, but the results wound up being a big noisy mess. Screenwriter Newman—who, in better times, collaborated on classics like *What's Up, Doc?* (1972) and *Bonnie and Clyde* (1967)—mostly abandons Santa Claus halfway through the movie for Patch (who keeps making puns of the "elf-improvement" variety) and BZ. (Apparently, neither Szwarc nor anyone else bothered to stop Lithgow, usually a fine actor, from madly chewing the scenery.) Add an uninvolving subplot about a rich little girl and poor little boy who befriend Santa, flagrant product placement for Mc-Donald's, and a production design that's an assault on the eyes (e.g., the elves all wear bright polka-dotted outfits), and you've got a trainwreck of Christmas movie that's so very wrong that you won't be able to tear yourself away from it.

**FUN FACTS**

- Directors who considered taking on the project, but dropped out for various reasons, included John Carpenter, Lewis Teague, Guy Hamilton, and Robert Wise. The Salkinds wound up going with Szwarc, who had previously directed their disastrous production of *Supergirl* (1984), not to mention the toothless *Jaws 2* (1978).
- Henry Mancini and Leslie Bricusse, who had previously collaborated on *Victor/Victoria* (1982), wrote the forgettable songs here. (Sheena Easton bleats, "It's Chriiiistmaaaas! All over the world tonight!" over the closing credits.) Bricusse fared much better with his holiday-themed songs and score for *Scrooge* (p. 151).
- Because of the film's *Superman* connection, smart alecks tweaked that earlier film's famous tag line to fit *Santa Claus: The Movie*— "You will believe a reindeer can fly." *Santa Claus'* real one was "Seeing is believing," which anyone who's actually watched the film can dispute.

## *Six Weeks* (1982)

PG; 107 min. Written by David Seltzer, based on the novel by Fred Mustard Stewart. Directed by Tony Bill. Starring Dudley Moore, Mary Tyler Moore, Katherine Healy. (Not currently available on DVD)

While on the campaign trail, politician Patrick Dalton (Dudley Moore) strikes up a friendship with young Nicole Dreyfus (Healy) and her mother Charlotte (Mary Tyler Moore), a wealthy cosmetics magnate. Nicole spends her time training as a dancer but begins applying her energy to Patrick's campaign. When Patrick wonders why Nicole isn't in school, Charlotte discloses that the girl has leukemia and isn't expected to live long. Eventually, Nicole convinces Patrick and Charlotte to take her to New York City for the holidays, even though this means more time that Patrick will spend far from his already-estranged wife and son. Nicole's dream to dance the lead role in *The Nutcracker* comes true when she's allowed to perform in a rehearsal at Lincoln Center, but will she survive the vacation? And can Charlotte and Patrick reconcile their feelings for each other when he's already got a family?

Oscar Wilde once observed that "one would have to have a heart of stone to read the death of Little Nell without laughing," and that's how I feel about this awful, goopy Christmas movie about a rich little girl who can feel the grim reaper breathing down her slender neck. As created by Healy, Seltzer, and Bill, Nicole Dreyfus is such a phony character—equal parts obnoxious precociousness and misty-eyed sentimentality—that you'll find yourself impatiently awaiting her demise. And Moore and Moore don't help matters, sparking all the chemistry of Dick Armey and Barney Frank between them; the fact that Dudley's character is technically philandering on his long-suffering wife doesn't make him any more likable. So why is *Six Weeks* worth a look? Because it's hilarious in that way that only bad movies dealing with super-serious subjects can be. In its way, *Six Weeks* was the vanguard of movies that milk easy tears with a death at Christmas. (It's surprising that no one thought to push that stupid Charlize Theron movie *Sweet November* [2001] back a month so that she could expire in Keanu Reeves' arms under the Christmas tree.) *Six Weeks* is the sort of film where dying of leukemia equals being completely healthy until that moment where the patient wails, "It hurts!" before suddenly dropping dead. (Think of it as the "cancer-as-teen-heart-attack" method.) Stir up a festive holiday punch, get your most gallows-humor-funny friends together, and catch *Six Weeks* on cable (or on an out-of-print VHS copy), and see if you don't spend weeks—maybe even more than six—impersonating Dudley Moore chiding Healy with a hammy, "You're an *outrageous* girl, Nicole!"

See also: The Christian-themed film *C Me Dance* (2009) also features a young ballerina with asymptomatic leukemia who drops dead at Christmastime. But first, she battles Satan! This inept drama is such a heavy-handed piece of proselytizing propaganda that even most devoted evangelicals would be embarrassed by it. The film is not without its share of unintentional laughs, but only the hardiest of souls could handle a *Six Weeks–C Me Dance* double feature.

## FUN FACTS

- Mr. Moore and Ms. Moore were coming off Oscar-nominated roles (Dudley in *Arthur*, Mary Tyler in *Ordinary People*), and Bill had just directed the popular *My Bodyguard*; the colossal critical and box-office flop of *Six Weeks* temporarily killed the career momentum of all three. As for Healy—cast because of her proficiency as a dancer—she never made another film, although she did graduate from Princeton in 1990 with a degree in Art History.
- This property went through many hands before finally hitting the screen. At one point it was Arthur Hiller directing Audrey Hepburn, Nick Nolte and Tatum O'Neal, but then Tatum hit puberty. At one point or other, actors connected to *Six Weeks* included Sylvester Stallone and Jacqueline Bisset; Paul Newman and Faye Dunaway; George Segal, Burt Reynolds, and as the kid, Quinn Cummings and Elizabeth McGovern.

## *Some of My Best Friends Are ... (1971)*

R; 110 min. Written and directed by Mervyn Nelson. Starring Gil Gerard, Fannie Flagg, Rue McClanahan, Candy Darling. (Not currently available on DVD)

It's Christmas Eve in a Manhattan gay bar, and all the sad and lonely men congregate for an evening of misery. A married businessman has a furtive and guilt-ridden rendezvous with his Swiss ski-instructor boyfriend. A disappointed mother, tipped off by the resident evil straight woman, slaps her son on the dance floor and tells him he's dead to her. An effeminate man meets the straight guy with whom he's had a relationship over the phone, only to face disappointment. A hustler, on the eve of a trip to Europe with his sugar daddy, savagely beats up a drag queen when he realizes she's not a biological woman. And so on.

If gay audiences thought *The Boys in the Band* (1970) was a depressing two hours of self-loathing, they'd soon discover that the adaptation of the Mart Crowley play was a cinematic pride parade compared to this exploitive drama that emerged the following year. In his landmark survey of gay characters in the movies, *The Celluloid Closet*, critic Vito Russo observes that *Some of My Best Friends Are ...* "is an enlightening period piece that has lost its power to offend"; indeed, a film that was once deemed "controversial" is so ridiculous and steeped in its own sense of poor-me-I'm-gay tragedy that it has transformed into a laugh riot over the years. Writer-director Nelson seems to have no affinity for either filmmaking or the characters he's presenting; Nixon-era gays loathed the film for presenting their urban lives as being full of despair, while modern gay audiences can't help laughing at all the teeth-gnashing and breast-beating on display.

See also: Alas, nobody has yet figured out how to make a great gay Christmas movie. The best of the lot is probably *Breakfast With Scot* (2007), which features a lovely holiday-set finale and a title character who's obsessed with Christmas; it's a cute movie that unfortunately tends to play like an extended sitcom pilot. There are some funny moments in *24 Nights* (1999)—and fun performances by Aida "sister of John" Turturro and Stephen "son of Norman" Mailer—about a love-hungry twenty-something who still believes in Santa, but the comedy's clunky direction accentuates its low-budget flaws. *Make the Yuletide Gay* (2009) features a handful of entertaining performances, but the script is weak and the Minnesota accents don't go with the Southern California locations. *Hollywood, je t'aime* (2009), about a French tourist looking for love and acting work in L.A., is just annoying, and the worst of the bunch would have to be the unbearable, shot-on-video *Visions of Sugarplums* (2001).

## FUN FACTS

- To give you some idea of how the media handled *Some of My Best Friends Are . . .* in 1971, the first paragraph of the *Variety* review includes the line, "Laden with every type of fag character, today's audience with this leaning should find it interesting fare." And from *Cue*: "[T]he denizens of the bar come on like mini-vaudeville acts, display their perversions, take their bows, and then swish off into the cold wintry night."
- Perhaps the most interesting facet of the film is the number of its cast members who would go on to find fame on the small screen. Gil Gerard (*Buck Rogers in the 25th Century*) plays a hunky gay pilot; Rue McClanahan (*Maude, The Golden Girls*) turns up as the villainous Lita Joyce; Fannie Flagg (the *Match Game* regular who would go on to write successful novels, including *Fried Green Tomatoes at the Whistle Stop Café*) shows up as the bar's hat-check girl; and *WKRP in Cincinnati*'s Gary Sandy made his film debut as Jim, the hustler. The cast also featured former MGM player Carleton Carpenter (he sang "Aba Daba Honeymoon" with Debbie Reynolds in 1950's *Two Weeks With Love*), Warhol superstar Candy Darling—who also pops up in *Silent Night, Bloody Night*

(p. 133)—and actor Calvin Culver, better known as gay porn star Casey Donovan.

## *Thomas Kinkade's Christmas Cottage* (2008)

PG; 96 min. Written by Ken LaZebnik. Directed by Michael Campus. Starring Jared Padalecki, Marcia Gay Harden, Peter O'Toole, Aaron Ashmore. (Lionsgate Home Video)

Young Tom Kinkade (Padalecki) travels home from college for Christmas vacation, only to discover that his mother Maryanne (Harden) is having a hard time making financial ends meet. Worried that Mom will lose her house next door to where Tom's mentor, artist Glen (O'Toole) lives—Tom looks for work in their small town and is eventually commissioned to create a mural that depicts their small town and its residents. Over the course of the holiday, Tom and his brother Pat (Ashmore) will be briefly reunited with their ne'er-do-well father Bill (Richard Burgi), the town will come together to create a Nativity pageant, and Tom will be inspired to, in the words of Glen, "Paint the light!"

If you thought the hideous, mass-produced "paintings of light" that turned the real Thomas Kinkade into a multimillionaire were awful, wait until you see this nauseating auto-hagiography that Kinkade and his wife produced. (By the same token, if you think Kinkade is a great artist, this just might be the movie for you.) Like *Santa Claus: The Movie* (p. 186), it's an origin story that's supposed to clue us in to the humble beginnings of this Great Man, but you don't have to loathe Kinkade's tacky artwork to think that this moronic film is hopelessly lodged up its own nether regions. Harden and O'Toole are both fine performers who deserve better than this codswallop, but not even they can keep this silly exercise in self-promotion from being anything but laughable from start to finish.

## FUN FACTS

- Author Joan Didion once described Kinkade's artwork as being "of such insistent coziness as to seem actually sinister, suggestive of a trap designed to attract Hansel and Gretel. Every window was lit, to lurid effect, as if the interior of the structure might be on fire." Another Kinkade critic, writer Susan Orlean, said of his paintings, "[They are] not quite real . . . as if painted by someone who hadn't been outside in a long time."

- *Vanity Fair* magazine published a memo featuring a list of 16 guidelines that Kinkade provided to the *Christmas Cottage* production, including "6) Hidden details whenever possible. References to my children (from youngest to oldest as follows): Evie, Winsor, Chandler and Merritt. References to my anniversary date, the number 52, the number 82, and the number 5282 (for fun, notice how many times this appears in my major published works). Hidden N's throughout— preferably thirty N's, commemorating one N for each year since the events happened." and "16) Most important concept of all—THE CONCEPT OF LOVE. Perhaps we could make large posters that simply say 'Love this movie' and post them about. I pour a lot of love into each painting, and sense that our crew has a genuine affection for this project. This starts with Michael Campus as a Director who feels great love toward this project, and should filter down through the ranks. Remember: 'Every scene is the best scene.'"

- Padalecki was signed to play Kinkade in a trilogy of films, each set in a different phase of the artist's life. Since *Thomas Kinkade's Christmas Cottage* was demoted from a theatrical release to a direct-to-video feature, it appears unlikely that the other two Kinkade films will ever be produced, much to the disappointment of bad-movie fans.

# CHAPTER 9

Thomas Mitchell (wearing scarf), Donna Reed, and James Stewart are surrounded by George Bailey's friends and family in *It's a Wonderful Life* (1946).

# Just Like the Ones I Used to Know

## CHRISTMAS CLASSICS

Here they are: The classics, the untouchables, the granddaddies of all Christmas movies. These are the unassailable favorites that win new fans every year and keep their admirers coming back December after December. The fact that a major television network will devote three hours of prime time to a black-and-white film from 1946 seems impossible in this day and age, but that's what NBC does for *It's a Wonderful Life* (p. 202)—twice a year, in fact. The other chapters in this book have sought to dig up movies that you might not think about in relation to Christmas—this chapter contains all the films that no Christmas movie guide could be without.

# *The Bells of St. Mary's* (1945)

**Unrated; 126 min. Written by Dudley Nichols; story by Leo McCarey. Directed by Leo McCarey. Starring Bing Crosby, Ingrid Bergman, Henry Travers. (Republic Pictures Home Video)**

Father O'Malley (Crosby, reprising the role that won him an Oscar for 1944's *Going My Way*) arrives at his new assignment, the crumbling St. Mary's school that's being run by a group of nuns led by Sister Mary Benedict (Bergman). O'Malley immediately learns that this new gig won't be an easy one—his predecessor got packed off to "Shady Rest" to recuperate. Grumpy millionaire Horace P. Bogardus (Travers) has bought the school's old playground and is erecting a skyscraper on it; Bogardus wants O'Malley to sell him the school so he can turn it into a parking lot, but the nuns are praying that they can convince Bogardus to give them his new building, since the school is so old and run-down that it's bound to be condemned (particularly since Bogardus has clout with the city). For the school to survive—and for this strong-headed priest to make peace with the stubborn Sister Mary Benedict—it's going to take a miracle.

Unabashedly sentimental, *The Bells of St. Mary's* scores cuteness points wherever possible, whether with twinkling nuns, a few songs by Crosby, the redemption of characters who seem past saving, or the sight of Bergman teaching a sensitive boy how to box. By the time the first-graders stage their adorable Christmas pageant, which ends with them singing "Happy Birthday to You" to baby Jesus, the movie has you in its grasp, and there's no escape. There's plenty to pick apart for those who are so inclined—McCarey and Nichols obviously side with O'Malley (who treats the nuns with a certain level of sexist condescension, even when Sister Mary is right and the priest is wrong), and describing the movie's overall style as "manipulative" is putting it mildly. Still, one has to acknowledge the power of this deftly crafted hokum; the movie boasts such a shrewd mix of the corny and the canny, bolstered by consistently winning performances, it's no wonder that *The Bells of St. Mary's* has become an annual tradition for its many admirers.

**FUN FACTS**
- *The Bells of St. Mary's* features a trio of Christmas movie all-stars: Crosby went on to star in *White Christmas* (p. 214); Joan Carroll, best known as second-youngest Agnes in *Meet Me in St. Louis* (p. 205), plays intelligent and troubled young Patsy; and Travers is, of course, most famous for his role as Clarence the angel in *It's a Wonderful Life* (p. 202).
- Speaking of *It's a Wonderful Life*, *The Bells of St. Mary's* is on the marquee in Bedford Falls when George Bailey runs by yelling, "Merry Christmas, movie house!"
- Crosby and Bergman performed two different radio adaptations of *The Bells of St. Mary's*, which aired in 1946 and 1947.
- Crosby and Bergman pulled a prank on the Catholic priest who was advising the production—they filmed an extra take of the final scene and ended it with a passionate kiss that made the cleric jump up in fury.

## *The Bishop's Wife* (1947)

Unrated; 109 min. Written by Leonardo Bercovici and Robert E. Sherwood, based on the book by Robert Nathan. Directed by Henry Koster. Starring Cary Grant, Loretta Young, David Niven, Monty Woolley. (MGM Home Video)

Bishop Henry Brougham (Niven) has become distracted from both his inner-city parish and his wife Julia (Young) because of his efforts to erect a huge cathedral. He asks heaven for guidance and gets Dudley (Grant), a charming angel who arrives to help. But Dudley's agenda has nothing to do with building the cathedral—he's there to remind Henry about what's really important in his life, and he does so by spending time with Julia (taking her to the restaurant where she and Henry used to go), working with the boys' choir at Henry's old church, and dazzling the crabby old millionaire (Gladys Cooper, as wicked here as she was as Bette Davis' monstrous mother in 1942's *Now, Voyager*) who's making Henry's life so difficult. Can Dudley get the Broughams' lives in order by Christmas? And will they even remember he was ever there?

There was something superhuman about Cary Grant's screen presence, so he's a perfect fit in this role of a celestial smooth operator who can do anything and who fixes people's lives without them even realizing that he's doing it. All the leads have challenging roles, but they make the most of them—Young reveals Julia's loving side without ever making the audience worry she's going to leave her husband for Dudley, and Niven allows hints of the good and kind man within to peek out, even when Bishop Henry is at his most brusque. It's a lovely little redemption story, handled with wit and grace—an ecumenical *Topper* (1937), if you will.

See also: *The Preacher's Wife* (1996) may lack some of the charm of the original—it's overlong and bland, with narration that's too cute by half—but any movie that allows Whitney Houston to sing gospel and Denzel Washington to channel Cary Grant can't be all bad. (Plus, it's got the irresistible Loretta Devine *and* Jenifer Lewis in supporting roles.)

## FUN FACTS

- Monty Woolley, who plays Henry and Julia's old friend Prof. Wutheridge, also stars in the Christmas-inclusive movies *Since You Went Away* (p. 94) and *The Man Who Came to Dinner* (1942).
- *The Bishop's Wife* had a guardian angel or two of its own. Producer Samuel Goldwyn had already spent $1 million on the project when he fired original director William A. Seiter and started over from scratch. Teresa Wright had been cast as Julia under Seiter,

but by the time shooting resumed under Koster, she had become pregnant and had to withdraw. Niven was to have played Dudley the angel, but after director Koster brought in Grant, who wanted the role, Niven was switched to the bishop. After early unsuccessful preview screenings, Billy Wilder and Charles Brackett contributed uncredited rewrites to the film. Not that any of this turmoil is reflected in the finished product.

## A Christmas Story (1983)

PG; 94 min. Written by Jean Shepherd, Leigh Brown, Bob Clark, based on Shepherd's *In God We Trust, All Others Pay Cash* and (uncredited) *Wanda Hickey's Night of Golden Memories.* Directed by Bob Clark. Starring Peter Billingsley, Darren McGavin, Melinda Dillon, Ian Petrella. (Warner Home Video)

Growing up in the 1940s, young Ralphie (Billingsley) wants nothing more than an official Red Ryder carbine-action 200-shot range model air rifle for Christmas, but his desires are thwarted at every turn by a chorus of adults telling him, "You'll shoot your eye out." He's got other childhood issues to deal with over the Christmas season, of course, from evil bully Scut Farkus (Zack Ward) to a "triple-dog-dare" that results in his friend Flick (Scott Schwartz) getting his tongue stuck on a frozen flagpole to the disappointment of a Little Orphan Annie decoder to getting a mouthful of soap from his mom (Dillon) when he accidentally curses in front of "the old man" (McGavin). *A Christmas Story* mixes the wonder and the terror of growing up in a way that evokes empathy, sympathy, and hilarity.

While this film was moderately successful in theaters, decades of constant exposure—including 24-hour marathons on cable television—have made *A Christmas Story* part of the common vernacular. Try tossing out phrases like "Fra-zhee-lay" or "How does the piggy eat?" to a roomful of Christmas revelers, and chances are they'll know exactly what you're talking about. Author Shepherd narrates the story of his own childhood—a style that would later be borrowed by TV's *The Wonder Years*—and the effect is not unlike spending time with an older relative of the raconteur variety, who perfectly remembers his childhood without leaving out either the good or the bad parts. Ralphie and his family have become as much a part of the communal Christmas experience as George Bailey and the denizens of Bedford Falls in *It's a Wonderful Life* (p. 202).

See also: Unbeknownst to many—since it was barely released to theaters—*A Christmas Story* has a sequel called *My Summer Story* (aka *It Runs in the Family*) (1994). Cast mostly with different actors, it's not nearly as fun or effective, although Mary Steenburgen stands out as the mother; when she and the other neighborhood ladies take out their wrath on the local movie theater manager, who has been stiffing them on their free commemorative movie-star china patterns, it's a sight to behold.

## FUN FACTS

- Special guns had to be created for the film, since the original Red Ryder rifles included neither a compass nor a sundial; in Shepard's memories, he apparently combined the Red Ryder with accessories available on the Buck Jones rifle.
- Director Clark's previous contribution to the Christmas movie genre was the terrifying *Black Christmas* (p. 126). He was able to make *A Christmas Story* without studio interference thanks to the success of his teen sex comedy *Porky's* (1982).
- *A Christmas Story* fan Brian Jones bought the house in Cleveland where exteriors of the film were shot, revamped the interiors to match the look of the film (the actual interiors were shot in a studio in Toronto), and has made the house a tourist attraction. (Winners of a charity auction have had the opportunity to spend Christmas Eve night in the house.) Jones also bought the house next door and turned it into a museum and gift shop; among the

items he sells there is a replica of the infamous "leg lamp" that Ralphie's dad wins as a "major prize."

- The film's intense fandom has led to a slew of documentaries, including the Bob Clark tribute *Clarkworld* (2009) and *Road Trip for Ralphie* (2008), about two Canadian fans who travel to all of the film's locations.

## *A Christmas Without Snow* (1980)

**Unrated; 95 min. Written by John Korty, Richard Beban, and Judith Nielsen; story by John Korty. Directed by John Korty. Starring Michael Learned, John Houseman, James Cromwell, Calvin Levels. (Echo Bridge Home Entertainment and other sources)**

Divorcée Zoe Jensen (Learned) moves to San Francisco in the hopes of getting work as a schoolteacher and making enough money so that her young son can leave her parents' house to come and live with her. Teaching jobs are hard to come by, so she gets by working secretarial gigs via a temp agency. As a way to meet people in this new city, Zoe gets involved with her church choir, where things are about to get exciting—legendary conductor Ephraim Adams (Houseman) has been hired as the new choral director, and this year, they're going to perform Handel's *Messiah*. Haughty soprano Mrs. Burns (Anne Lawder) storms out when she isn't given a solo, the church organ gets vandalized, and there's dissension in the ranks—can these amateur singers get it together to perform this complicated piece of music in time for Christmas?

Many Christmas movies go for the grand gesture and the sweeping redemption—Scrooge, for one, transforms from London's biggest miser to the nicest man in town, all in one night—but *A Christmas Without Snow* gives us smaller triumphs, more life-sized life lessons, and a powerful sense of community. While Zoe spends much of the film far away from home and family, she comes to create a new family for herself among the eccentric and kind-hearted choir members whom she comes to love. Houseman (who gives a lovely speech explaining why "amateur" is a term of praise and not a pejorative) once again plays a demanding taskmaster, but his Ephraim possesses a droll sense of humor and an abiding love of music; he proves to be the kind of uncompromising but caring teacher we all hope to be lucky enough to have at some point in our lives. (Is this made for TV movie a classic? I think so, if only because for most of the people I mentioned this one to, even if they didn't remember the title, the plot rang a bell and they thought of it fondly. It's always been one of my favorites, too.)

**FUN FACTS**

- The director of several acclaimed TV movies—including the Emmy-winning *The Autobiography of Miss Jane Pittman* (1974), starring Cicely Tyson, who would later play the lead in his *Ms. Scrooge* (p. 159)—Korty won an Oscar for his 1977 documentary *Who Are the DeBolts? (And Where Did They Get 19 Kids?)*. He established a San Francisco–based production facility in the late 1960s, inspiring both George Lucas (who produced Korty's 1983 animated feature *Twice Upon a Time*) and Francis Ford Coppola (who executive-produced Korty's 1972 TV movie *The People*) to do likewise. David Fincher later worked for Korty before becoming a filmmaker himself.

- *A Christmas Without Snow* debuted on CBS on December 9, 1980. The film has since lapsed into the public domain—it is easily obtainable from a number of DVD companies, and even for free streaming online, but the video quality differs widely from source to source.

# It's a Wonderful Life (1946)

**Unrated; 130 min. Written by Frances Goodrich, Albert Hackett, and Frank Capra; additional scenes by Jo Swerling; based on the story "The**

Greatest Gift" by Philip Van Doren Stern. Directed by Frank Capra. Starring James Stewart, Donna Reed, Lionel Barrymore, Henry Travers. (Paramount Home Entertainment)

Clarence (Travers), an angel who hasn't earned his wings, learns all about the life of George Bailey (Stewart) so that he can help the man on the darkest night of his life. George dreamed of seeing the world, but wound up staying in his small town of Bedford Falls, N.Y., to run his father's Building and Loan company, lest the city's crotchety rich man Mr. Potter (Barrymore) take over all the local businesses. George falls in love with Mary (Reed) and raises children with her, and under his direction, the Bailey Building and Loan builds homes for lots of working-class people in town who never thought they could afford one. One Christmas Eve, George's dotty Uncle Billy (Thomas Mitchell) accidentally hands Potter a copy of the newspaper that happens to have $8,000 of the Building and Loan's money in it, and when Billy fails to make the deposit, Potter accuses George of embezzling from the company. George contemplates suicide, but when Clarence shows him how awful everything would have been in Bedford Falls had George never been born, the distraught small-town banker comes to appreciate the value of his life.

In his essential film guide *Cult Movies*, Danny Peary observes that "*It's a Wonderful Life* is the most reassuring film: not only do you (whom George represents) have a family who loves you, a hometown sweetheart who loves you and marries you, a guardian angel who loves you and protects you, but also you have an entire town of people who love you and come to your aid when you are in trouble—in today's world, when your next-door neighbor only comes to your door to tell you to keep the noise down, this is a wonderfully comforting image." As with Capra's *Meet John Doe* (p. 97), *It's a Wonderful Life* represents a battle between a man of the people (George) and a rich and powerful villain (Potter) for the very souls of the masses. Over the course of the film, we get to know and love George, which is why it's so painful to see him reach the end of his tether and, worse, to see how miserable the lives of everyone around him would have been in his absence. By the time, the story reaches its hyper-emotional climax, it's a sweeping ending that's been fully earned; we need an overwhelming catharsis to cap off the emotional rollercoaster we've been on. Like Ebenezer Scrooge (Chapter 7) and Kevin from *Home Alone* (p. 6), George has gotten a glimpse of another existence that makes him appreciate his present circumstances, and that's a lesson that most of us enjoy learning all over again every Christmas.

## FUN FACTS

- Thomas Mitchell, who plays sweet, scatterbrained Uncle Billy, was actually one of the actors in consideration to play mean old Mr. Potter. But Lionel Barrymore got the role, at least in part because of the popularity of his Scrooge in radio versions of *A Christmas Carol* at the time.

- Jimmy the Raven, the pet bird who lives at the Bailey Building and Loan, also appeared in Capra's Oscar-winning *You Can't Take It With You* (1938) and in every post-*Wonderful Life* Capra movie.

- A financial disappointment in its original release, the film busted Capra's production company Liberty Films, which made only one other movie (the 1948 Hepburn-Tracy political drama *State of the Union*). *It's a Wonderful Life* didn't reach classic status until it went into the public domain and became a ubiquitous television staple in the 1970s and '80s. (The film's copyright has since been renewed.)

- The original screenplay began with a scene in Benjamin Franklin's workshop in heaven; this was later discarded in favor of the talking constellations that open the film.

- The story on which the film was based, Philip Van Doren Stern's "The Greatest Gift," was one that its author couldn't get published, so he sent it out as a Christmas card instead. That's how it landed on the desk of a producer at RKO.

- RKO developed a special chemical snow for the film so that actors' voices could be recorded while they walked on it; prior to that, movies used crushed cornflakes.
- The swimming pool that opens up under a dancing George and Mary still resides in the gym at Beverly Hills High School. And that's Carl Switzer—best known as "Alfalfa" in the *Our Gang* shorts—as Mary's jilted escort.
- Despite the Christmas theme of the film, *It's a Wonderful Life* opened in theaters in January.
- *It's a Wonderful Life* won no Oscars, and out of its five nominated categories, it was bested in four of them by *The Best Years of Our Lives*, a darker take on post-war America.
- The *Sesame Street* characters of Bert and Ernie were not, despite appearances, named after the cop and the cab driver in the film; according to Muppet insiders, it's just a coincidence.
- Yes, Marlo Thomas starred in a made-for-TV remake called *It Happened One Christmas* (1977). Let us never speak of it again.

## *Meet Me in St. Louis* (1944)

**Unrated; 113 min. Written by Irving Brecher and Fred F. Finklehoffe, based on the novel** *5135 Kensington* **by Sally Benson. Directed by Vincente Minnelli. Starring Judy Garland, Margaret O'Brien, Mary Astor, Lucille Bremer. (Warner Home Video)**

The 1904 World's Fair is still a year away, but the Smith family of St. Louis can hardly wait for this international event to come to their hometown. In the meantime, they've got plenty to keep them busy: Second-oldest Esther (Garland) has fallen in love with John Truett (Tom Drake), who just moved in next door; oldest daughter Rose (Bremer) hopes she'll soon be engaged; and youngest Tootie (O'Brien) always manages to get herself into trouble, no matter what the season. Just before Christmas, Mr. Smith (Leon

Ames) drops a bombshell: He's accepted a promotion that will take him to New York City, and the whole family will be leaving St. Louis at the beginning of the year. Will the rest of the Smith clan be ready to leave behind their lives, their friends, and their beloved hometown?

When people get sentimental about "the good old days," they're imagining some slice of perfection along the lines of what happens in *Meet Me in St. Louis*. And even if we know that nobody's life was ever as idyllic as the Smiths', we can nonetheless dream of Christmas balls and trolley rides and Halloween pranks and everything else that happens over the course of this adorable, kind-hearted film. Garland gives one of her greatest screen performances under the direction of Minnelli, whom she would soon marry, and the film stands among the peak achievements of MGM's Freed Unit, which was also responsible for such classics as *Singin' in the Rain* (1952) and *Gigi* (1958). *Meet Me in St. Louis* launched two songs that would become standards: "The Trolley Song" and "Have Yourself a Merry Little Christmas," and no vocalist since Garland has ever threatened her ownership of these tunes.

**FUN FACTS**

- Most cover versions of "Have Yourself a Merry Little Christmas" remove the song's more poignant elements. In the film, Esther sings it to Tootie to try and cheer her up about their impending move, but it contains lines like "Until then, we'll have to muddle through somehow" and "Next year, all our troubles will be miles away"; a few singers perform the song as originally written, but most later renditions make the song cheerier than it was in its original context.

- A Broadway adaptation, featuring additional songs, opened in November of 1989. Cast members who believed the run wouldn't last took to calling the show "I'll Be Home for Christmas," but it remained open until June 1990.

- *Meet Me in St. Louis* figures in two films starring Sarah Jessica Parker; in *The Family Stone* (2005), one of the characters is watching the "Have Yourself a Merry Little Christmas" number, and in *Sex and the City* (2008), Parker's Carrie Bradshaw watches "The Trolley Song" alone on New Year's Eve.

## *Miracle on 34th Street* (1947)

**Unrated; 96 min. Written by George Seaton; story by Valentine Davies. Directed by George Seaton. Starring Edmund Gwenn, Natalie Wood, Maureen O'Hara, John Payne. (20th Century Fox Home Entertainment)**

When the Macy's Thanksgiving Day Parade Santa gets drunk, store higher-up Doris Walker (O'Hara) gets lucky with the sudden appearance of Kris Kringle (Gwenn), who steps in at the last minute. Kringle is such a great Santa—he even brings his own costume— that he gets a full-time job at Macy's. Kringle, however, insists that he's the real Santa, much to the chagrin of store psychologist Mr. Sawyer (Porter Hall). As for Doris' precocious daughter Susan (Wood), she doesn't believe in Santa at all, having been raised by Doris to see the world in absolutes; Kris eventually teaches Susan to use her imagination for the first time. Kris becomes the subject of a sanity hearing, and lawyer Fred Gailey (Payne)—Doris' next-door neighbor, who is courting her—goes all-out to prove that his client is none other than the real Santa Claus.

*Miracle on 34th Street* is loaded with so many lovely character-based moments—Kris' honesty in the Santa chair inspiring a new Macy's policy, to send customers to Gimbels or other stores if they can find better prices; Susan letting her guard down for the first time and pretending to be a wild animal; the families of the prosecuting attorney and the judge getting angry over Daddy putting Santa on trial—that it's obvious that the filmmakers didn't just rely on their high-concept plot to get them through. We want Kris to prevail, for Doris and Fred to get together, for Susan to allow herself to be a child and to believe in Santa, and it's that desire that brings us back to this sweet family film every December. Skip the charmless remakes—the 1994 version written by John Hughes is probably the least terrible, while the 1973 TV-movie is downright noxious—and insist on the genuine article.

## FUN FACTS

- After the film's release, the real Macy's hired a "Christine Kringle" who would direct shoppers to better bargains at other stores.
- Gwenn received a well-deserved Best Supporting Actor Oscar for his role as Kris Kringle.
- *Miracle on 34th Street* was given a B ("morally objectionable") rating by the United States Conference of Catholic Bishops for its favorable depiction of a divorced woman.
- Operating under the notion that more people went to the movies during the summer rather than at Christmastime, Fox chief Darryl Zanuck downplayed the Santa Claus angle in the film's promotion—and released it in May of 1947.
- If the name of actor Porter Hall sounds familiar, it might be because Roger Ebert and Russ Meyer borrowed it for one of the characters in *Beyond the Valley of the Dolls* (1970). The real Hall also appeared in *Double Indemnity* and *Going My Way* (both 1944) and *Ace in the Hole* (1951), among many others.
- Veteran character actress Thelma Ritter makes her screen debut in *Miracle on 34th Street* as the mother who becomes a devoted Macy's customer after Kris sends her to another store.
- That's the real 1946 Macy's Thanksgiving Day Parade featured early in the film; Gwenn actually played the parade's Santa that year.
- In the unsubtitled sequence where Kris talks to a refugee Dutch girl in her language, she tells him that she doesn't want anything, since being adopted by her new mother was already gift enough.

# *The Nightmare Before Christmas* (1993)

PG; 76 min. Written by Caroline Thompson; adapted by Michael Mc-Dowell; story by Tim Burton. Directed by Henry Selick. Starring Chris Sarandon, Danny Elfman, Catherine O'Hara, Glenn Shadix. (Walt Disney Home Video)

Jack Skellington (speaking voice, Sarandon; singing voice, Elfman) is the Pumpkin King and ruler of Halloween Town, where everything is spooky and everyone works all year round to make Halloween the scariest holiday of them all. Jack finds that he's getting tired of Halloween and longs for something different. One night he takes a walk and discovers the portals to other holidays, and when he finds Christmas, he's thoroughly enchanted. He tries explaining snow and presents and Santa Claus to the other denizens of Halloween Town, but they don't quite get it. Nonetheless, Jack decides to kidnap "Sandy Claws" (Ed Ivory) and to take over Christmas this year. The results, naturally, are disastrous, and only Santa can save the day—provided he can escape the clutches of the monstrous Oogie Boogie (Ken Page), who has dastardly plans for Father Christmas.

This dazzling combination of the merry and the macabre has so quickly become such a holiday perennial that it's hard to remember when the idea of combining Halloween and Christmas in one movie seemed inconceivable. But Tim Burton's dark vision—brilliantly executed by stop-motion master Selick (2009's *Coraline*)—makes these vastly different holidays go together like candy canes and popcorn balls. Elfman's songs mirror the movie's unlikely combination, mixing cheery, minor-key tunes like "What's This?"—sung by Jack when he's delighted and confused over the sights of Christmas Town—and dark compositions like "Kidnap the Sandy Claws." It's the movie that made it safe for people to hang bats and goblins on their Christmas tree, and *Nightmare* has become an integral, if innocently ghoulish, part of the last three months of the year.

See also: The middle of Burton's Christmas trilogy, after *Batman Returns* (p. 104) and before *The Nightmare Before Christmas*, is *Edward Scissorhands* (1990), a lovely, haunting fable about Edward (Johnny Depp), a boy who just wants to fit into everyday life but has to contend with, well, his scissorhands. The scene in which he uses his sharp fingers to carve ice sculptures at Christmastime—making it snow in a sunny neighborhood—ranks among the most breathtaking sequences in any of Burton's films.

**FUN FACTS**

- *Nightmare* was based on a poem Burton wrote in the early 1980s; after his animated short *Vincent* (1982) became popular, Disney considered turning the poem into a short or a TV special. (Burton says the poem was inspired by seeing Halloween decorations coexisting with Christmas decorations in a store window when one display was being replaced with the other.)
- There were nearly 800 Jack Skellington heads, to convey a panoply of emotions.
- The Walt Disney Company originally released *Nightmare* under its Touchstone Pictures banner, fearing it would be too frightening for children. The 3-D re-release in 2006 (and every year since) has gone out with the Walt Disney Pictures logo.
- Since 2001, Disneyland in Anaheim, Calif., has themed its Haunted Mansion attraction with characters from *The Nightmare Before Christmas* every year at the holidays.
- The villainous Oogie Boogie was inspired by a character played by Cab Calloway in the Betty Boop short *The Old Man of the Mountain* (1933).
- Jack Skellington makes brief appearances in Burton's *Vincent* and *Beetlejuice* (1988), in the latter as part of the lead character's carousel hat. (He also turns up later in Selick's 1996 animated adaptation of Roald Dahl's *James and the Giant Peach*.)

- Vincent Price was originally cast as Santa Claus, but his failing health and weak voice made his recordings unusable. Price died on October 25, 1993, just four days before *Nightmare*'s theatrical release.

## *The Shop Around the Corner* (1940)

Unrated; 99 min. Written by Samson Raphaelson, based on the play *Parfumerie* by Nikolaus Laszlo. Directed by Ernst Lubitsch. Starring James Stewart, Margaret Sullavan, Frank Morgan, Joseph Schildkraut. (Warner Home Video)

Co-workers Klara (Sullavan) and Alfred (Stewart), both clerks at an upscale Budapest boutique at the turn of the 20th century, despise each other, but they unknowingly exchange breathlessly romantic letters as pen pals. There's no shortage of intrigue at the store, owned by Mr. Matuschek (Morgan), whose wife is cheating on him—he incorrectly believes Alfred may be cuckolding him, not realizing that his wife's lover is someone else on his payroll. When Alfred loses his job over the misunderstanding, he's too depressed to keep his date with his pen pal, but after a friend peeks in and tells him that Klara is the girl he was supposed to meet, Alfred has to decide whether or not to declare his love to his rival. Whatever happens between Alfred and Klara, it's going to have to wait until after the Christmas rush.

Even today, filmmakers strive to achieve what's known as the "Lubitsch touch" in romantic comedies—Billy Wilder actually kept a framed banner in his office that read, "How would Lubitsch do it?"—and the master's skill at juggling fully formed characters, snappy dialogue, and the perfect dollop of sentimentality is fully on display in this classic. While the film makes little effort to hide its stage-bound origins, the performances are so sparkling and the chemistry among all the characters (not just the leads, who have it by the stocking-full) is so sharp that you won't mind spending time inside Matuschek's. (William Tracy steals scene after scene as the store's harried errand boy.) Workplace comedies and contentious romances as delightful as *The Shop Around the Corner* come around all too rarely.

See also: The film has been remade twice, to varying degrees of success. *In the Good Old Summertime* (1949) seems clearly designed to put Judy Garland back into a picture hat after the success of *Meet Me in St. Louis* (p. 205), and while it has its charms, Van Johnson is definitely no Jimmy Stewart. And then there's *You've Got Mail* (1998), starring Tom Hanks and Meg Ryan as rival booksellers who become internet chat buddies; nice try, but no cigar.

**FUN FACTS**

- Throughout the production of the film, Lubitsch was inspired by memories of his father's shop in Berlin. The director later called this "the best picture I ever made in my life."
- Charles Smith has a brief appearance at the end of the film as Matuschek's new errand boy. Smith would turn up later as a member of a barbershop quartet in *In the Good Old Summertime*. (The latter movie's most famous cameo appearance would have to be the screen debut of three-month-old Liza Minnelli, who appears in the final moments alongside her mother.)
- The Broadway musical *She Loves Me* and the long-running British sitcom *Are You Being Served?* are both based on the same source material as *The Shop Around the Corner*.

## *We're No Angels* (1955)

Unrated; 106 min. Written by Ranald MacDougall, based on the plays *My Three Angels* by Samuel and Bella Spewack and *La Cuisine des Anges* by Albert Husson. Directed by Michael Curtiz. Starring Humphrey Bogart, Peter Ustinov, Aldo Ray, Joan Bennett. (Paramount Home Entertainment)

Prisoners Joseph (Bogart), Jules (Ustinov), and Albert (Ray) escape from Devil's Island. Hoping to find cash and new clothes before hopping a steamship back to Europe, the trio cases a store owned by Félix Ducotel (Leo G. Carroll), who lives in back with his wife Amélie (Bennett) and daughter Isabelle (Gloria Talbott). The criminals find themselves moved by the family's plight—the Ducotels are deeply in debt to, and under the thumb of, Félix's cruel cousin André Trochard (Basil Rathbone). On top of that, Isabelle is in love with André's nephew Paul (John Baer), although André has already arranged for him to be married to a young woman of means. The escaped prisoners will use their larcenous skills—with the assistance of a poisonous snake named Adolphe—to make this Christmas a merry one for the Ducotel family.

Ustinov and Ray are playing murderers, and Bogie's an embezzler, but the convicts' interaction with each other is so droll and "No, ahftah *you*" that it's quickly established that this film takes place in a cloud-cuckooland of its own, where desperate escapees from the world's most wretched prison will put aside their plans of flight to do a good deed for some nice people. If you're willing to suspend your disbelief enough to make the story work, *We're No Angels* offers a bounty of witty dialogue, holiday-season redemption, and old-fashioned movie-star charm. (This is one of a handful of movies that, during my childhood, made my household drop whatever they were doing and gather around the TV set, at any time of year.) Rathbone once again shows why he's considered one of the great screen rotters, Bennett gives as good as she gets in her scenes with Bogart, and Ustinov underplays hilariously. You'll be amazed how much fun you'll have spending Christmas in sunny French Guyana with three escaped felons.

## FUN FACTS
- Talbott is best known to fans of genre cinema for her roles in *I Married a Monster From Outer Space* (1958) and *Girls Town* (1959)

before becoming a regular guest presence on series television throughout the 1960s.

- Director Curtiz released this film back-to-back with another holiday favorite, *White Christmas* (see below).
- Screenwriter David Mamet and director Neil Jordan made a 1989 comedy called *We're No Angels*. It is not set at Christmas. Nor is it funny.

## White Christmas (1954)

**Unrated; 120 min. Written by Norman Krasna, Norman Panama, and Melvin Frank. Directed by Michael Curtiz. Starring Bing Crosby, Rosemary Clooney, Danny Kaye, Vera-Ellen. (Paramount Home Entertainment)**

While fighting in World War II, PFC Phil Davis (Kaye) rescues song-and-dance man Bob Wallace (Crosby) from certain death; by playing upon Wallace's guilt and sense of obligation, Davis worms his way into the showman's act. They wind up being a big hit as a duo; years later, while in Florida, they check out a performance by the Haynes Sisters, Betty (Clooney) and Judy (Vera-Ellen), whose brother is an old war buddy of Bob and Phil's. Phil, desperately trying to marry off workaholic Bob and sensing an attraction between Bob and Betty, insists that they follow the girls to a holiday engagement in snowy Vermont. When they arrive, they discover two surprises: The weather is balmy, and the hotel where the Haynes sisters are booked to perform is owned by Bob and Phil's wartime commanding officer, retired General Waverly (Dean Jagger). Bob comes to the hotel's financial rescue by bringing his entire show to stay at the hotel and rehearse over Christmas, but he also wants to boost the spirits of the general, who's feeling old and useless. Bob goes on TV to rally the soldiers from his division to surprise the general on Christmas Eve, but Betty assumes that Bob is exploiting the old soldier for publicity. Can the lovers reunite in time for the big show? And will sunny Vermont have a white Christmas?

"White Christmas," the classic Irving Berlin song, is all about nostalgia—the tune became a hit during World War II because it resonated among soldiers fighting overseas and longing for a holiday "just like the ones I used to know." *White Christmas*, the movie, is about the nostalgia those same soldiers, now safely at home, had for the Great War they had fought just a decade earlier. The film falls firmly into the genre of musicals about show people, with many of the song-and-dance numbers presented as rehearsals for the Wallace and Davis show, and it effortlessly blends sentimentality with energetic performances and some genuine chemistry among three of the four leads. (Let's just say that as an actress, Vera-Ellen is an exceptional dancer.)

See also: *Holiday Inn* (1942), the film in which Crosby first introduced the song "White Christmas" to the world, makes for a tricky recommendation. On the one hand, it's a terrific musical, packed with great Irving Berlin songs and some dazzling footwork from Fred Astaire. (At one point, he does a July 4 routine that involves exploding firecrackers.) On the other hand, there's the "Abraham" number, which involves Crosby and Marjorie Reynolds wearing blackface and pretending to be liberated slaves. (The film's actual African American characters are old-school caricatures as well.) If you skip over those parts—or are prepared to give your children a brief explanation of the history of American racism—there are enough high points to *Holiday Inn* to make it worth watching, but it's the blackface scene that keeps the movie from being shown on television as frequently as it used to be. (*White Christmas* doesn't include any blackface, but there is a big number that pays tribute to "minstrel shows.")

**FUN FACTS**

- As *White Christmas* proudly states up front, it was the first film to be shot in VistaVision, a widescreen process that Paramount hoped would rival Fox's CinemaScope. It was also filmed in rather vivid Technicolor—Crosby's famous blue eyes and the redredRED Santa outfits in the final number all but threaten to scorch the screen.

- That's future Oscar winner (for 1961's *West Side Story*) George Chakiris as one of Clooney's four backup dancers in the "Love, You Didn't Do Right by Me" number. Other notables who turn up briefly are Barrie Chase, who appeared opposite Astaire in a series of acclaimed 1960s TV specials, as the "mutual, I'm sure" girl; Sig Ruman, one of the three Russian envoys in *Ninotchka* (1939), as a crooked landlord; and veteran character actors Percy Helton and Grady Sutton as, respectively, the train conductor and an obstreperous party guest.

- Fred Astaire was originally considered for the Danny Kaye role. Then Crosby and Astaire both left the project (Crosby didn't want to make a movie so soon after his first wife Dixie's death, and when he left, so did Astaire) before Crosby eventually returned.

- Part of the legend behind director Curtiz's classic film *Casablanca* was that it was being constantly rewritten during the shoot, with no one knowing until the end of production whether Ilsa would stay with Rick or get on the plane with Victor. Similarly, *White Christmas* screenwriters Melvin Frank and Norman Panama (who had just written *Knock on Wood* for Danny Kaye) were frantically rewriting Norman Krasna's original script even after the sets and choreography were in place and the cast was drawing salary. Years later, Frank told an interviewer, "Writing that movie was the worst experience of my life. Norman Krasna was a talented man, but I told Michael Curtiz that it was the lousiest story I'd ever heard. It needed a brand-new story, one that made sense and had plenty of sentimentality. It was so tough, and we were so tired. We literally wrote seven days and seven nights a week for eight weeks."

- You can't hear the songs from *White Christmas* exactly the way they were sung on screen, with the same singers, anywhere outside of the film; Clooney was under exclusive contract to Columbia Records, so she did her own album of them. The "official" *White Christmas* soundtrack album recorded for Decca Records had Crosby, Kaye, and Trudy Stevens (who sang for Vera-Ellen in the movie) singing alongside a youngster named Peggy Lee, performing Clooney's parts. Both versions are now available on CD.

James Gandolfini and Ben Affleck in *Surviving Christmas* (2004).

# Appendix

Movies that I didn't get to in the main part of the book, either because they feature Christmas so very briefly, or because they were good but didn't quite fit, or because they were bad but not fun-bad, just bad-bad. (I didn't include TV movies, which would require their own separate volume, although a few made-for-TV movies are cited elsewhere in this book.) This is by no means not a complete list, so if I left out your favorite, remember that this is the season for forgiveness.

Films with a * are recommended, but not necessarily as Christmas movies.

*9 Songs* (2004)
*101 Reykjavík* (2000)
*2046* (2004)*
*400 Blows, The* (1959)*
*1900* (1976)*
*1941* (1979)

*Addams Family, The* (1991)
*Affair to Remember, An* (1957)*
*Aguirre, the Wrath of God* (1972)*
*Alice* (1990)

*All Fall Down* (1962)*
*All I Want for Christmas* (1991)
*All That Heaven Allows* (1955)*
*Alvin and the Chipmunks* (2007)
*Amen.* (2002)
*American Gangster* (2007)
*American Psycho* (2000)
*American Romance, An* (1944)
*Angela's Ashes* (1999)
*Annie Hall* (1977)*
*Anywhere but Here* (1999)
*Associate, The* (1996)
*Au revoir, les enfants* (1987)*
*Auntie Mame* (1958)*
*Away From Her* (2006)*

*Babe* (1995)*
*Babes in Toyland* (1934)*
*Baby Face* (1933)*
*Baby Formula, The* (2008)
*Beaches* (1988)
*Bed of Roses* (1996)
*Behind Enemy Lines* (2001)
*Bell Book and Candle* (1958)*
*Beloved Infidel* (1959)
*Best Defense* (1984)
*Beyond Silence* (1996)
*Big Eden* (2000)*
*Bill of Divorcement, The* (1932)
*Billy Elliot* (2000)*
*Black Narcissus* (1947)*
*Bless the Child* (2000)
*The Blind Side* (2009)

*Blossoms in the Dust* (1941)

*Blow* (2001)

*Bone Collector, The* (1999)

*Boogie Nights* (1997)

*Bourne Identity, The* (2002)

*Bush Christmas* (1947)

*Butterflies Are Free* (1972)


*C.R.A.Z.Y.* (2005)*

*Captain Newman, M.D.* (1963)

*Cast Away* (2000)

*Catch Me if You Can* (2001)

*Charlotte's Web* (2006)*

*Chasing Liberty* (2004)

*Chattahoochee* (1989)

*Cheaper by the Dozen* (2003)

*The Children* (2008)

*Christ Stopped at Eboli* (1979)

*Christine* (1983)

*Christmas Eve* (1947)

*Christmas in July* (1940)*

*Christmas in the Clouds* (2001)

*Christmas Martian, The* (1971)

*Christmas Tree, The* (1969)

*Christmas With the Kranks* (2004)

*Chronicles of Narnia: The Lion, the Witch, and the Wardrobe, The* (2005)*

*Citizen Kane* (1941)* (Orson Welles jumps decades between young
   Kane saying, "Merry Christmas," and his guardian Mr. Thatcher
   responding, "And a Happy New Year!")

*City of Lost Children* (1995)*

*Click* (2006)

*Cobra* (1986)

*Cold Mountain* (2003)

*Color Purple, The* (1985)*
*Come See the Paradise* (1990)
*Communion* (1989)
*Convicts* (1991)
*Coup de grâce* (1976)
*Crash* (2004)
*Croupier* (1998)*
*Curse of the Cat People* (1944)*

*Day Mars Invaded Earth, The* (1963)
*Day of the Beast* (1995)
*Day of the Locust, The* (1975)*
*Dead Bang* (1989)*
*Dead of Night* (1945)*
*Deal of the Century* (1983)
*Dear God* (1996)
*December Boys* (2007)
*Deck the Halls* (2006)
*Deep Red* (1975)
*Destination Tokyo* (1943)
*Digging to China* (1998)
*Dillinger* (1945)
*Diner* (1982)*
*Dondi* (1961)
*Donnie Brasco* (1997)*
*Donovan's Reef* (1963)
*Don't Open 'Til Christmas* (1984)
*Doubt* (2008)
*Douce* (1943)*
*Down to the Bone* (2004)*
*Driving Miss Daisy* (1989)
*Dry White Season, A* (1989)
*Duplex* (2003)

*Eastern Promises* (2007)
*Edward II* (1991)*
*Elmer Gantry* (1960)*
*End of Days* (1999)
*Enemy of the State* (1998)
*English Patient, The* (1996)
*Entrapment* (1999)
*Evelyn* (2002)
*Everybody's Fine* (2009)
*Everyone Says I Love You* (1996)*

*Falling in Love* (1984)
*Family Man, The* (2000)
*Family Stone, The* (2005)
*Far From Heaven* (2002)*
*Fast Times at Ridgemont High* (1982)*
*Ferpect Crime, The* (2004)
*Field of Dreams* (1989)*
*First Blood* (1982)
*First Daughter* (2004)
*Fitzwilly* (1967)
*Flannel Pajamas* (2006)
*Fortune and Men's Eyes* (1971)
*Frozen River* (2008)
*Friends With Money* (2006)*
*Four Christmases* (2008)
*Fred Claus* (2007) (Pretty awful, but Paul Giamatti makes a terrific
    Santa.)
*Full Metal Jacket* (1987)*
*Funny Farm* (1988)*

*Giant* (1956)*
*Glenn Miller Story, The* (1954)

*Godfather, The* (1972)*
*Godfather, Part II, The* (1974)*
*Gods and Generals* (2003)
*Gone With the Wind* (1939)*
*Goodfellas* (1990)*
*Grand Illusion* (1937)*
*Greatest Show on Earth, The* (1952)
*Greystoke: The Legend of Tarzan, Lord of the Apes* (1984)
*Grumpy Old Men* (1993)

*Hard 8* (aka *Sydney*) (1996)
*Hardcore* (1979)
*Harry Potter and the Sorcerer's Stone* (2001)*
*Heavenly Creatures* (1994)*
*Hellboy II: The Golden Army* (2008)
*Holiday* (1938)*
*Holiday, The* (2006)
*Hook* (1991)
*Hope and Glory* (1987)*
*Hot Rods to Hell* (1967)
*Hotel New Hampshire, The* (1984)
*House of the Spirits* (1993)
*How the Grinch Stole Christmas* (2000)
*Howards End* (1992)*
*Hulk* (2003)
*Hush* (1998)

*I Am Legend* (2007)*
*I Come in Peace* (1990)
*If Ever I See You Again* (1978)* (A wonderfully horrible ego project
    from songwriter Joe Brooks of "You Light up My Life" fame, who
    also directs, writes, and stars.)
*I'll Be Home for Christmas* (1998)

*Imitation of Life* (1959)*
*In Bruges* (2008)*
*Incredible Shrinking Woman, The* (1981)
*Infamous* (2006)
*Intervista* (1987)
*Invasion U.S.A.* (1985)
*Inventing the Abbotts* (1997)

*Jacket, The* (2005)
*Jaws: The Revenge* (1987)
*Jingle All the Way* (1996)
*Johnny Got His Gun* (1971)
*Johns* (1996)

*Kramer vs. Kramer* (1979)

*Lady and the Tramp* (1955)*
*Lady in White, The* (1988)
*Land Girls, The* (1998)
*Last American Virgin, The* (1982)
*Last Holiday* (2006)
*Last Night* (1998)*
*Last Picture Show, The* (1971)*
*Last Time I Committed Suicide, The* (1997)
*Lemon Drop Kid, The* (1951)* (This Bob Hope comedy, based on a
    Damon Runyon story, introduced the song "Silver Bells.")
*Let Him Have It* (1991)
*Life With Mikey* (1993)
*Live Flesh* (1997)*
*Long Walk Home, The* (1990)*
*Look Who's Talking Now* (1993)
*Looking for Mr. Goodbar* (1977)
*Love Finds Andy Hardy* (1938)*

*Lovers on the Bridge, The* (1991)*
*Lucky Numbers* (2000)

*Ma and Pa Kettle at Home* (1954)
*Maid in Manhattan* (2002)
*Mame* (1974) (Wherein the staying power of composer Jerry Herman's "We Need a Little Christmas" is confirmed by Lucille Ball's inability to destroy it.)
*Man Bites Dog* (1992)*
*Man of a Thousand Faces* (1957)
*Man on the Moon* (1999)
*Man Who Came to Dinner, The* (1942)
*Maniac* (1980)
*Matador, The* (2005)
*Maurice* (1987)*
*Max* (2002)
*McCabe & Mrs. Miller* (1971)*
*Mean Girls* (2004)*
*Merry Gentleman, The* (2008)
*Michael* (1996)
*Midnight in the Garden of Good and Evil* (1997)
*Midwinter's Tale, A* (1995)
*Miracle* (2004)
*Miracle of Morgan's Creek, The* (1944)*
*Miss Potter* (2006)
*Mixed Nuts* (1994) (If this isn't the single worst Christmas movie of all time, it's at least an astonishing waste of comic talent—how can a movie starring Steve Martin, Madeline Kahn, Rita Wilson, Anthony LaPaglia, Juliette Lewis, and Liev Schreiber, with supporting bits by Parker Posey, Jon Stewart, Garry Shandling, and Adam Sandler be this utterly miserable? We're talking not-a-single-laugh unfunny.)
*Mommie Dearest* (1981)*

*Money Train* (1995)
*Mortal Thoughts* (1991)
*Morvern Callar* (2002)*
*Mothman Prophecies, The* (2002)
*Mouth to Mouth* (1995)*
*Mr. & Mrs. Bridge* (1990)
*Mr. Woodcock* (2007)
*Muertos de risa* (1999)*
*My Father's Glory* (1990)*
*My Favorite Season* (1993)*
*My Mother's Castle* (1990)*
*Mysterious Skin* (2004)*

*Nativity Story, The* (2006) (Yes, I know, a book about Christmas
   movies probably should have spent more time on this one, but
   frankly, I found it difficult to stay awake while watching.)
*Nénette et Boni* (1996)*
*Nickelodeon* (1976)*
*Night Sun* (1990)
*No Man's Land* (1987)
*Noel* (2004)
*Notes on a Scandal* (2006)*
*Notorious Bettie Page, The* (2005)*
*Nun's Story, The* (1959)

*O. Henry's Full House* (1952)
*Ocean's Eleven* (1960)
*Old Maid, The* (1939)*
*Once Around* (1991)*
*One Hour Photo* (2002)
*One Magic Christmas* (1985)
*One True Thing* (1998)
*Ordinary People* (1980)*

*Oscar and Lucinda* (1997)*
*Outside Providence* (1999)

*P2* (2007)
*Package, The* (1989)
*Painted Hills, The* (1951)
*Paradise Alley* (1978)
*Party Monster* (2003)
*Paul Blart: Mall Cop* (2009)
*Penny Serenade* (1941)*
*Perfect Holiday, The* (2007)
*Performance* (1970)*
*Period of Adjustment* (1962)*
*Persepolis* (2007)*
*Peter's Friends* (1992)*
*Peyton Place* (1957)*
*Pirate Radio* (2009)
*Pocketful of Miracles* (1961)
*Polar Express, The* (2004)
*Postcards From America* (1994)*
*Pranks* (aka *The Dorm That Dripped Blood*) (1982)
*President's Analyst, The* (1967)*
*Pride and Glory* (2008)
*Proposition, The* (2005)
*Puberty Blues* (1981)*

*Quai des orfèvres* (1947)*

*'R Xmas* (2001)
*Radio* (2003)
*Raising Arizona* (1987)*
*Reckless* (1995)
*Reds* (1981)*

*Reindeer Games* (2000)

*Rent* (2005)

*Riding in Cars With Boys* (2001)

*RoboCop 3* (1993)

*Rocky* (1976)*

*Rogue Trader* (1999)

*Ronin* (1998)

*Rosemary's Baby* (1968)*

*Rover Dangerfield* (1991) (for containing that immortal doggie urina-
tion anthem, "I'd Never Do It on a Christmas Tree")

*Rushmore* (1998)*


*Santa Claws* (1996)

*Santa With Muscles* (1996)

*Santa's Slay* (2005)

*Saved!* (2004)*

*Say One for Me* (1959)

*Scenes From a Mall* (1991)*

*Serendipity* (2001)

*Seven Little Foys, The* (1955)

*Shadowlands* (1993)

*Shaft* (1971)*

*Show Boat* (1951)*

*Sid and Nancy* (1986)*

*Simon Birch* (1998)

*Sleeping Dictionary, The* (2003)

*Slipping-Down Life, A* (1999)

*Smart People* (2008)

*Smoke* (1995)*

*So Proudly We Hail!* (1943)

*Soldier* (1998)

*Some Mother's Son* (1996)

*Someone Like You . . .* (2001)

*Stalag 17* (1953)*
*Starter for 10* (2006)
*Starting Over* (1979)*
*Steel Magnolias* (1989)
*Stella Dallas* (1937)
*Stepmom* (1998)
*Storm Warning* (1951)
*Story of Alexander Graham Bell, The* (1939)
*Strange Days* (1995)*
*Summer Place, A* (1959)*
*Sunshine* (1999)*
*Surveillance* (2006)
*Surviving Christmas* (2004) (Starts strong, but you can tell the exact moment where the notes from studio executives take over, completely sucking the life out of the movie)
*Survivors, The* (1983)
*Swiss Family Robinson, The* (1960)*

*Tall Guy, The* (1989)
*Taras Bulba* (1962)
*Tenth Avenue Angel* (1948)
*They Live by Night* (1948)*
*Thin Man, The* (1934)*
*Those Who Love Me Can Take the Train* (1998)*
*Together* (2000)*
*Tommy* (1975)*
*Torch Song Trilogy* (1988)*
*Toy Story* (1995)*
*Trading Places* (1983)
*Trouble With Angels, The* (1966)*
*Truman Show, The* (1998)*
*Trust the Man* (2005)

*Turbulence* (1997)
*Twelve Monkeys* (1995)

*Umbrellas of Cherbourg, The* (1964)*
*Under Suspicion* (2000)
*Under the Tuscan Sun* (2003)
*Untamed Heart* (1993)

*Vera Drake* (2004)
*View From the Top* (2003)

*War of the Roses, The* (1989)*
*We of the Never Never* (1982)*
*Welcome to L.A.* (1976)
*What a Way to Go!* (1964)*
*When Harry Met Sally . . .* (1989)*
*While You Were Sleeping* (1995)
*Whole Wide World, The* (1996)*
*Will Penny* (1968)
*Willard* (2003)
*Winter Sleepers* (1997)
*Without You, I'm Nothing* (1989)*
*World of Henry Orient, The* (1964)*

*Year of the Dog* (2007)
*Young Man With a Horn* (1950)*
*Yours, Mine and Ours* (1968)

*Zed and Two Noughts, A* (1985)*
*Zentropa* (1991)*
*Zodiac* (2007)*

Margaret O'Brien and Judy Garland in *Meet Me in St. Louis* (1944).

# Index of Names

# Index of Titles